Physical Characteristics of the Keeshond

(from the American Kennel Club breed standard)

Tail: Moderately long and well feathered, set on high and tightly curled over the back. It should lie flat and close to the body. The tail must form a part of the "silhouette" of the dog's body, rather than give the appearance of an appendage.

Body: Compact with a short, straight back sloping slightly downward toward the hindquarters: well ribbed, barrel well rounded, short in loin, belly moderately tucked up, deep and strong of chest.

Hindquarters: Angulation in rear should be between slight to moderate to complement the forequarters, creating balance and typical gait. Hindquarters are well muscled with hocks perpendicular to the ground.

Size: Medium-sized, square-appearing, sturdy dog, neither coarse nor lightly made. The ideal height of fully matured dogs when measured from top of withers to the ground is 18 inches for males and 17 inches for bitches; a 1-inch variance either way is acceptable.

Feet: Compact, well rounded, cat-like. Toes are nicely arched, with black nails.

Keeshond

By J. Piet Hessel

Contents

Training Your Keeshond **83**

Begin with the basics of training the puppy and adult dog. Learn the principles of house-training the Keeshond, including the use of crates and basic scent instincts. Enter Puppy Kindergarten and introduce the pup to his collar and leash and progress to the basic commands. Find out about obedience classes and other activities.

Healthcare of Your Keeshond **107**

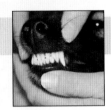

By Lowell Ackerman DVM, DACVD
Become your dog's healthcare advocate and a well-educated canine keeper. Select a skilled and able veterinarian. Discuss pet insurance, vaccinations and infectious diseases, the neuter/spay decision and a sensible, effective plan for parasite control, including fleas, ticks and worms.

Your Aging Keeshond **138**

Know when to consider your Keeshond a senior and what special needs he will have. Learn the signs of aging in terms of physical and behavioral traits and what your vet can do to optimize your dog's golden years. Consider some advice about saying good-bye to your beloved pet.

Showing Your Keeshond **146**

Step into the center ring and find out about the world of showing pure-bred dogs. Here's how to get started in AKC shows, how they are organized, and what's required for your dog to become a champion. Take a leap into the realms of obedience trials, agility, earthdog events and tracking tests.

KENNEL CLUB BOOKS: **KEESHOND**

ISBN: 1-59378-327-2

Photography by Isabelle Français, Karen Taylor and Alice van Kempen,

with additional photographs by
Paulette Braun, T.J. Calhoun, Alan and Sandy Carey, Carolina Biological Supply, Bill Jonas, Dr. Dennis Kunkel, Tam C. Nguyen, Phototake and Jean Claude Revy.

Illustrations by Patricia Peters.

The publisher wishes to thank all of the owners whose dogs are illustrated in this book.

How long did it take for the Northern Wolf to emerge from the forest? Ask the wolf-gray Keeshond.

HISTORY OF THE
KEESHOND

CANINE EVOLUTION

Modern research leaves little doubt that, by various steps and crosses, most breeds of dog have descended from *Canis lupus*, the wolf. The descent was primarily from the northern branch of the family known as the northern European gray wolf.

Just how long it took for the wolf to come out of the forest and join man in his dwelling remains a point of conjecture. However, we are nearly certain that it took place gradually and that it came about through early man's observation and appreciation of the wolf's many social habits and effective hunting techniques. The social aspects of the wolf struck a familiar note with man. Archeological discoveries indicate that man easily could have learned to copy the wolf's hunting techniques as well. The association grew from there, and it also appears that domestication led to the wolf's offering assistance in the hunt itself.

The wolves that could assist in satisfying the unending human need for food were, of course, most highly prized. It also became increasingly obvious, as the man/wolf relationship developed through the ages, that certain descendants of these increasingly domesticated wolves could be used by man to assist in other survival pursuits in addition to hunting. Also highly valued were those wolves that were large enough to assist in hauling. Nor would man overlook the value of the wolf-*cum*-dog that voiced some kind of warning sound when a marauding neighbor or beast of prey threatened.

Through the centuries, many descendants of the original wolf stock were to acquire great anatomical changes with man's intervention and breeding manipulation. However, long before man began to manipulate the size and shape of *Canis familiaris* (the domestic dog), there existed a branch of the family Canidae that, because of its close proximity to wolf ancestry, retained many of the wolf's physical characteristics.

Like their undomesticated wolf ancestors, these dogs maintained the characteristics that protected them from the rugged environment of northern Europe. Their weather-resistant coats protected the dogs from both rain and cold. The long coarse outer coat was able to shed snow and rain, and a dense undercoat helped to insulate against sub-zero temperatures. These coats were especially abundant around the neck and chest, thereby offering double protection for the vital organs.

The Nordic dogs' noses and mouths could be covered and protected by their heavily plumed tails when they were forced to sleep in the snow. Small furred prick ears were not easily frost-bitten or frozen. The muzzle had sufficient length to warm the frigid air before it reached the lungs. Leg length was sufficient to keep the chest and abdomen above the snow line. Tails were carried horizontally or up over the back rather than trailing behind in the snow.

Skeletal remains of these early wolf descendants have been found throughout northern and central Europe, northern Asia and the Arctic regions of North America. They stand as the forerunners of what are

---

HOW TO SAY IT

There are two fully acceptable pronunciations of the Keeshond's breed name. The most popularly used is *caze-hawnd* (plural, Keeshonden, pronounced *caze-hawnd-en*). The other is *case-hawnd* (plural, *case-hawnd-en*). Subtle differences, yes, but advocates of each are staunch in their beliefs and just might offer correction. Never, on the other hand, should the breed name be pronounced *kees-hound* or *kees-hounds*!

commonly referred to as the Arctic or Nordic breeds.

This group can be divided effectually into four categories: hunting dogs (examples: Elkhound, Chow Chow and Karelian Bear Dog), draft dogs (Alaskan Malamute, Siberian Husky), herding dogs (Samoyed, Swedish and Finnish Lapphunds) and companion dogs (Keeshond, German Spitz, Japanese Spitz, Volpino Italiano and most of the other spitz-type dogs).

One specific branch of this family was known as *Canis familiaris palustris*, or more commonly and interchangeably known as both "the dog of the lake" and "peat bog dog." Skeletons of these spitz-type dogs have been found in many places throughout northern Europe and are said to have existed in the late Stone Age. While the dogs' exact roles in the lives of the tribes cannot be fully identified, some cynologists and breed historians suggest that the dogs lacked hunting instincts but may have served as watchdogs. They offered protection, not in the aggressiveness of a modern-day guard dog but in sounding the alarm by barking when danger threatened. The alert nature, rapid vocal response and protective devotion to home and hearth of today's spitz breeds certainly give credibility to this theory.

The Norwegian Elkhound.

The Finnish Lapphund.

The Nordic breeds, or spitz dogs, possess key similarities, including their double, weather-resistant coats, prick ears, curled tails, pointed muzzles and alert dispositions.

The German Spitz (Mittel).

THE SPITZ BREEDS IN GERMANY

The spitz breeds had already become popular in Germany by the early 1500s. Count Eberhard zu Sayne, a nobleman who resided in the Rhine Valley, is the first to have been known to refer to the dogs as "spitz." The word *spitz* is German for "sharp point," obviously referring to the dogs' characteristic pointed muzzle. The Count described the dogs as having no real interest in hunting but as being totally dedicated to their masters and protecting home and property. Evidently the Count had great influence in Germany in that from his first use of the term "spitz" in 1540, the word was included not only in the German vocabulary but also in dictionaries from that point on.

The dogs came in many sizes and many colors, each being identified by a separate name within Germany. As the dogs migrated outside Germany's borders to surrounding countries, yet other names were given to dogs that were obviously of the same character and heritage. Sometimes the name referred to the particular duties assigned to the dogs. At other times the breed or variety's name was the result of the town or province in which the breed was developed.

All of these spitz dogs, however, shared the same physical characteristics that had distinguished them for many centuries prior. For our purposes here, it is probably most useful to look at how the Germans separated the varieties by size. This classification system was used originally in Germany and is that which is used today by the Fédération Internationale Cynologique (FCI), which is the canine governing authority throughout Europe.

The Wolfspitz is the largest of the five German spitz breeds. It stands approximately 18 or more inches at the shoulder. The only color allowed is gray. The next size

BOTTOM LEFT: The German Spitz (Klein) has long been overshadowed by the equally diminutive but eminently popular Pomeranian. BOTTOM RIGHT: A parti-colored variety of the German Spitz (Klein), showing how colorful this charming small spitz can be.

The German Wolfspitz, the largest of the country's spitz breeds, is the German equivalent of the Keeshond of Holland. The two breeds are indistinguishable except in name and place of origin.

is the Grossspitz, sometimes called the Giant Spitz, which stands 40.5 cm (16 in) and above at the shoulder. Colors are white, black, brown and orange.

The Mittelspitz or Standard Spitz is ideally 29–35.5 cm (11.5–14 in) and can be white, black, brown, wolf gray or orange. The Kleinspitz or Small Spitz is bred in white, black, brown, wolf gray and orange and measures 23–28 cm (9–11 in). The Zwergspitz (Dwarf Spitz) can be white, black, brown, wolf gray or orange, and measures less than 21 cm (8.5 in).

It is the largest, or German Wolfspitz, that we are primarily concerned with here. In France, this variety was known as Chiens Loup, in Italy as the Lupini, in the UK as the Dutch Barge Dog and in Holland as the Keeshond (pronounced *caze-hawnd*; the plural, Keeshonden, pronounced *caze-hawnd-en*).

THE KEESHOND GETS ITS NAME

Often the Keeshond is referred to as the Dutch Barge Dog. The barge referred to was a large vessel that stood somewhere in size between a tug boat and a freighter. A barge moved easily on rivers and canals throughout the Netherlands. When necessary, the vessels ventured out into the far reaches of a bay or fjord, but they were not ocean-going vessels. The Keeshond was often kept aboard these barges as sentries and to keep the rodent population at bay.

NOT A HUNTER

Hunting was never taken up by the Dutch people; their national breed, the Keeshond, follows suit. Historically the breed has never exhibited a hunting instinct and therefore can easily be compatible with almost any other household pet.

CANIS LUPUS

"Grandma, what big teeth you have!" The gray wolf, a familiar figure in fairy tales and legends, has had its reputation tarnished and its population pummeled over the centuries. Yet it is the descendants of this much-feared creature to which we open our homes and hearts. Our beloved dog, *Canis domesticus*, derives directly from the gray wolf, a highly social canine that lives in elaborately structured packs. In the wild, the gray wolf can range from 60 to 175 pounds, standing between 25 and 40 inches in height.

In the late 1700s, the Keeshond was very well thought of in the Netherlands and the breed flourished throughout the land. This was particularly the case in the southern provinces of Brabant and Limburg. It was there that the breed was taken on as mascot of the common Patriot Party, which opposed those who supported the Prince of Orange as governor of the Netherlands.

The rebellious "Patriots" were led by Cornelius ("Kees") de Gyselear, and it was Kees's own "hond" (dog) that became the emblem of the Patriot party and from which the breed was to derive its proper name.

Unfortunately for all concerned, it was the House of Orange that was to emerge victorious in the political struggle, and the Patriot Party slipped into general disregard along with their Keeshonden, which were then considered affiliates of the defeated. In fact, many of the breed were destroyed by their owners in order not to appear to be Patriot sympathizers.

Only country folk farmers and those who operated the barges that proliferated in the Netherlands retained any loyalty to the breed. For a full century, the gentle and devoted Keeshond languished in obscurity, serving primarily in their appointed duties as watchdogs and vermin controllers on the river boats, barges and farms.

However, Miss J. G. Van der Blom and later the Baroness van Hardenbroek came upon the scene, took the breed in hand and, through their efforts, revived interest in the Keeshond. Miss Van der Blom showed her first Keeshond in 1891 in Amsterdam. The breed's beauty and success in the show rings attracted more fanciers and led to the importation of more stock from Germany. The breed's admirers established the Nederlandse Keeshond Club in 1924.

The success of Baroness van Hardenbroek's breeding program was creating interest both at home and throughout the Continent and England. A staunch supporter of the breed, the Baroness led the resistance to Germany's attempts to have the breed officially called the German Wolfspitz in the Netherlands. Her adamant dedication to the Keeshond name and her resistance to any change influenced the breed club that was established in England in 1925.

Originally called the Dutch Barge Dog, the Keeshond began turning heads at Kennel Club shows in the 1920s, when fanciers admired the breed's bespectacled eyes and commanding appearance.

THE KEESHOND IN BRITAIN

The Keeshond grew in popularity in its homeland and, under the guidance of talented breeders, quality continually improved. One of these influential breeders was Mrs. Alice Gatacre, who would eventually emigrate to England after her marriage.

At first the Keeshond was looked upon simply as an "overweight Pomeranian" in England. Some not-too-exceptional specimens of the breed were shown in the late 1800s, but they had only limited success. Though initially offered Challenge Certificates (CCs), required for championship in the UK, the breed was withdrawn from eligibility and was not to be heard from again until the 1920s, when it reappeared on The Kennel Club's roster of breeds eligible for CCs as Dutch Barge Dogs.

In the interim, Mrs. Gatacre and Mrs. Winfield Digby spearheaded some interest in the breed, but it was not until 1905, and almost by chance, that a major kennel for the breed was established. In that year, a young Miss Hamilton-Fletcher was yachting with her parents in Holland. There she was to meet and fall in love with the dogs that she saw standing proudly on the many barges that the travelers passed as the family traversed the country's canals.

Miss Fletcher was so intrigued that she was compelled to look into the history and temperament of the breed and by the time she returned to England she had purchased two puppies that became treasured members of her household.

Later, as the married Mrs. Winfield Digby, the former Miss Fletcher established her Van Zaandam Kennel at Sherborne Castle in Dorset. Through her devotion to the breed and prowess as a breeder, Mrs. Digby earned herself a revered place in the history and development of the breed.

WORKS OF ART

Many spitz-type dogs that resembled the Keeshond achieved popularity in the 18th century and can be found in the work of notable artists of the period, including portraits by the celebrated Gainsborough. The dogs portrayed, however, were known as "foxdogs" or "overweight Pomeranians." The name Keeshond was not officially used until 1920s.

Her Van Zaandam breeding force was made up of more dogs she imported from Holland and others she found in Germany. Shown first as Dutch Barge Dogs, the Van Zaandam dogs were of such outstanding quality that they soon drew the attention of pure-bred dog aficionados throughout England.

In 1925, breed fanciers organized the Dutch Barge Dog Club and elected Mrs. Digby as president. Registrations totalled 25. In 1926, the breed was officially given the Keeshond name, and a standard was drawn up that has withstood the test of time and has been used as a model throughout the world.

The Van Zaandam breeding program grew from strength to strength and, in 1929, Dochfour Hendrik, a dog owned by Baroness Burton and bred by Mrs. Digby, became the first Keeshond to earn its championship in England. Mrs. Digby's own Gesina Van Zaandam became the first female champion. Both of these champions were products of Mrs. Digby's Dutch-German bloodlines.

The Keeshond was extremely fortunate to have supporters of the breed whose talents ranged over the entire gamut of abilities that assisted the rapid development of the breed in England. There is no doubt that Mrs. Alice Gatacre's emigration from

Holland was a boon to the breed. Her literary efforts describing the many attributes of the Keeshond were extremely influential in bringing the many fine characteristics of the breed to the attention of the general public.

Mrs. Gatacre and her Guelder Kennel were not alone in supporting the cause of the breed. She was joined by a host of fanciers whose enthusiasm paralleled Mrs. Gatacre's and whose breeding programs also produced dogs that were great assets to the breed.

THE BARGE DOG IN THE US

The level of quality produced by these breeders not only took England by storm but also began to attract the attention of fanciers throughout the world. America was to lead the host of international fans who were to take up the cause of this new and lovely breed.

The Keeshond breed was literally unknown in America until the first dogs were registered with the American Kennel Club in 1930. The first litter born in the US was whelped in 1929 by Carl Hinderer of Maryland, a German immigrant whose efforts led to the breed's recognition by the American Kennel club (AKC). Evenlode, Vorden, Wistonia, Rhinevale, Sandar and Duroya were among the kennel names that had great influence not only in England but also in America.

Wistonia particularly influenced the breed in America through the exportation of a number of dogs that proved to be extremely formidable competition in American show rings. Not only did the Wistonia dogs acquire a notable roster of championships in their homeland, they proved extraordinary competitors in American and Canadian Breed, Group and Best in Show rings.

The Keeshond Club of America was founded in 1935 (originally called the Keeshond Club) in Chestnut Hill, Pennsylvania. Mrs. Irving Florsheim of the Red Top Kennels, one of the earliest Kees breeders in the US, served as the first president. Two years later the club held its first specialty show in Long Island, New York, which Ch. Herzog of Evenlode, owned by Mrs. Richard Fort, was selected as Best of Breed by judge Oliver C. Harriman.

Although the Keeshond is not used as a hunting or field dog today, the breed is more than willing to participate in outdoor activities and enjoys the great outdoors as much as the next barge dog!

In the US the breed established its footings on the East coast with the Ruttkay Kennels of Mrs. Virginia Ruttkay of Connecticut in 1946, a breeder whose influence continues decades after her death. Many kennels successfully used the Ruttkay Kees such as Sahnsirai (owned by Bill and Betty Ginsberg) Fairville (owned by Marcie Goebel), Modesto (owned by Floyd and Blanche Matthews) and Brynhaven (owned by Linda Louck) as well as the current Ruttkay Kennels in Reading, Pennsylvania (owned by Audrey A. Bostwick). Other important East-coast kennels include Wynfomeer (owned by Betty Dunn-Cummings), Sherwood (owned by Phyllis Noonan), Larah (owned by Sarah Louie), Van Ons (owned by Mrs. Richard Koehne), Vandy (owned by Carole Henry), KeesLund (owned by Tony and Judy Pomato), and Bearpaws (owned by Marcy Zingler).

The breed grew in popularity in the Midwest as well, with many foundation kennels springing up in Ohio and Michigan as well as Wisconsin, Missouri and Illinois. Among the early Midwestern kennels are Holland Hond (owned by Harriet Cinkosky), Mar-I-Ben (owned by Marilyn Bender and Eloise Geiger), Denwood (owned by Sue T. Rucker), Tanglewood (owned by Carol J. Aubut), Kalmia

---

ELIZABETHAN STYLE
The luxurious ruff that frames the head, neck and shoulders of the Keeshond strikes a reminiscent note of clothing worn during the Elizabethan period. Some fanciers attribute this as a good reason for the breed's popularity in Britain.

(owned by Irene Fonseca and Maryellen Grace), Ronson's (owned by Ron and Judy Fulton), Candray (owned by George and Jan Wanamaker), Graywyn (owned by Jo-Ann Gray), Yank-Kee (owned by Peter and Holly Colcord) and GreenKees (owned by Bill and Tess Eckhart).

Finally, the Western US caught Keeshond fever, and there the breed became an overnight sensation. Most West-coast breeding is linked to the Flakkee Kennels, owned by Mr. and Mrs. Porter Washington of California, whose records in showing and breeding are admired by all breeders in the fancy even today. The Flakkee dogs became the foundation of many West-coast kennels, including Star-Kees (owned by Robin Stark), Shamrock (owned by Shannon Kelly), Windrift (owned by Joanne Reed) and Travelers (owned by Sandy Krueger). Flakkee achieved many distinctions over the years, not the least of which was the first American-bred Best in Show winner, Ch. Patriot van Fitz, bred by Vera Fitzpatrick and owned by Flakkee Kennels. Mrs. Washington also owned the first two Keeshond bitches to take a Best in Show in the US, Eng. & Am. Ch. Whimsy of Wistonia (1949) and Eng. & Am. Ch. Wrona of Wistonia (1951). Another legendary Kees from Flakkee was Eng., Am. & Can. Ch. Wrocky of Wistonia, whose 1955 show record of 18 Bests in Show in 11 months was regarded as a landmark achievement. Wrocky enhanced the image of the Keeshond and attracted many new fans to the breed. Indeed he may have been the greatest Keeshond the breed has ever known. Ch. Flakkee Sweepstakes, aptly named "Sweeper," swept his way through nearly 50 Best in Show awards in the late 1960s, not to mention 2 specialty shows.

Other West-coast breeders include Jee Jac (owned by Jean and Jack Howard), located in Washington; Tyron (owned by Jean Ellis), founded in the late 1960s on Flakkee dogs; Wistonia, the famous British kennel's new home in California; Star-Kees, (owned by Robin Stark), home of the famous Batman, sire of 50 AKC champions; Shamrock (owned by Shannon Kelly); Fearless (owned by Joe and Helen Cuneo); Windrift (owned by Joanne Reed) and ABC (owned by Arleen Grimes).

The Keeshond is at home on land or water, having worked on large boats as watchdogs and exterminators.

From coast to coast, the Keeshond today has achieved renown in show rings, garnering Group placements and Best in Show ribbons on a regular basis. The hundreds of active American kennels, as well as the many regional clubs, represent a breed in strong, loving hands. All modern-day Keeshond breeders, exhibitors and owners, whose dogs go back to these foundation kennels and dogs, must revere the dedication and success of these pioneer Kees folk. Were it not for their commitment and hard work, we would not have such handsome bespectacled Dutch fellows with which to share our lives.

Whether a puppy or an adult, the Keeshond requires grooming for his luxuriant coat to keep it looking magnificent and healthty.

ARE YOU READY FOR A KEESHOND?

Is the Keeshond the best breed of dog for you and your family? Will this bespectacled spitz and you see eye to eye? Will the dog fit into your lifestyle and home environment? Let's consider these and other important concerns as we look at the characteristics of the Keeshond.

Very large and rambunctious dogs are hardly a suitable choice for the elderly, nor would they be a good choice for toddlers who are still unsteady on their feet. Tiny dogs or very young puppies are not a wise choice for families with children who have not yet learned how delicate these little creatures are. A full-grown Kees can handle the rough-and-tumble play of young children, while a very young Kees puppy may not be a good idea for a household in which the children have had no experience in dealing with baby animals.

Then too there is the matter of hair. A luxuriously coated dog is certainly beautiful to behold, but all that hair takes a great deal of care. Grooming an adult Keeshond in full coat takes about one hour to thoroughly brush, but when the dog is shedding, it can take even longer. Neglecting

PUPPY IQ

Even the youngest Keeshond puppy is very smart and will learn very quickly that crying at night brings all the attention he wants if you respond to it. The puppy will be just as quick to learn that naughty behavior brings about your disapproval and that dreaded "no" word.

the Kees's abundant coat would be subjecting your spitz beauty to uncomfortable tangles and mats and would be a sacrilege to this noble animal.

Regular bathing can be difficult for some owners. It can be tedious to thoroughly wash and rinse the breed's dense coat, and drying it without the proper equipment is almost impossible. If this procedure cannot be done properly at home, it must be

done by a professional groomer at least every two months. Although professional assistance takes care of the bathing and grooming problem, please understand that good and reliable groomers are not always available around the corner nor do their services come free of charge.

As great as claims are for a Kees's intelligence and trainability, remember that all new dogs, whether tiny puppies or fully mature adults, must be taught every household rule that they will be expected to observe. Although a Kees is able to catch on very quickly, it does not necessarily follow that every lesson will be one that the individual dog wants to learn. Puppies are just as inclined to forget or disregard lessons as young children.

CASE FOR THE PURE-BRED DOG

Why all this fuss and deliberation? Isn't it just as easy to go to the local animal shelter and select an attractive puppy of some kind? While all puppies are cute, not all puppies grow up to be particularly attractive adults. What is considered to be beautiful by one person is not necessarily seen as even remotely attractive by another.

It is almost impossible to determine what a mixed-breed puppy will look like as an adult.

LEADER OF THE PACK

One of the most critical time periods for you and your Keeshond is that between 12 and 16 weeks of age. During that time the puppy will find out who the pack leader in the family is. There are only two possibilities: you or your puppy. It is extremely important that the owner establish and maintain the correct relationship during this period.

Nor will it be possible to determine if the mixed-breed puppy's temperament is suitable for the person or family who wishes to own him. If the puppy grows up to be too big, too hairy or too active for the owner, what then will happen to it?

Size and temperament can vary to a degree even within pure-bred dogs. Still, selective breeding over many generations has produced consistent, typical dogs, giving the would-be-owner reasonable assurance of what the pure-bred puppy will look and act like as an adult. Aesthetics completely aside, this predictability is more important than one might think.

Pure-bred puppies will grow up to look like their adult relatives and, by and large, they will behave pretty much like the rest of their family. Please understand that practically any dog, mixed breed or not, has the potential to be a loving companion. However, the predictability of a pure-bred dog offers reasonable insurance that it will suit not only the owner's lifestyle but also that person's esthetic qualifications.

Before you bring a Keeshond puppy into your household, visit breeders and spend as much time with both puppies and adults as you can. Be sure that the adult Kees is the dog that appeals to you aesthetically and temperamentally.

GOOD TO SEE YOU!
The Kees will save his very special form of greeting for those he particularly loves, especially when the object of his affection has just returned from an absence. At those times a Kees will leap high into the air while shaking his head and emitting snorts and sneezes.

PERSONALITY AND TEMPERAMENT
The Keeshond has many wonderful personality traits and some that might be difficult to cope with for the wrong owner or the

COMPANION *PAR EXCELLENCE*

The Keeshond today is primarily a companion dog, though the breed is especially adaptive for Hearing Ear programs for the deaf. Because of their attentive, alert natures and their deep affection for humans, Keeshonden excel in social work and love to be involved with humans. They make excellent therapy dogs for hospitals and nursing homes.

owner who is not careful to keep some of those characteristics under control when the dog is still young. This is not to say that an older dog cannot be retrained, but it is a far less difficult job to teach a puppy Kees what is and isn't wanted than it is to convince the adult Kees that something he has always done is no longer permitted.

Historically, the Keeshond was bred and developed as a watchdog and, therefore, he is very alert and has an acute sense of hearing. The breed is instinctively quick to warn you about visitors or intruders. One Kees owner told us that his dog's hearing was so highly developed that the Keeshond heard things before they even happened!

There are some breeds that never utter more than a whimper, and even that on rare occasions. A Kees is not and is not likely to ever be one of those dogs! On the other hand, a responsible owner can and must teach his Kees that barking for no reason at all is not acceptable.

With their high degree of intelligence, Keeshonden tend to get bored easily. These are not dogs that can be left on their own continuously or kept outdoors alone. They are "people dogs" and, denied the opportunity to be with those they love, Kees can demand attention by becoming barkers. One of the breed's finest qualities is its desire to bond with and please its master. Not being allowed to do so can make even the best-bred Kees unhappy and hard to live with.

The two Keeshond characteristics that are particularly misunderstood and can be perceived as threatening by people unfamiliar with the breed are the Keeshond's "smile" and the breed's habit of "talking." The smile, actually a sign of submission, can be seen as a challenging snarl by the uninitiated when it is actually nothing of the sort. Kees "talk" can be misunderstood as a growl. His growl comes from down deep in the chest, whereas talking is done higher in the throat. The best way to differentiate between the two is in the dog's body language. When a Keeshond is having a "conversation" with you or anyone else, you will be able to observe the dog's entire being involved. Sparkling eyes and wagging tail, in fact, the whole body of the Kees gets into the act when he has something to say!

The need to be close to his master is very strong in the Keeshond. In fact, he can be underfoot just when you have forgotten he is there, which can be dangerous for someone who is not agile! But this need is born out of love and there is never any doubt that your Kees loves you. His love is absolutely uncondi-

LOVE APPLAUSE!
Keeshonden love the spotlight and relish applause and praise. To watch a Keeshond flying over a jump at an agility trial or strutting his double-curled tail in the show ring is to see a happy dog that loves the attention that public events bring the breed. Some breeds do not welcome the crowds and the noise, but the Keeshond is one that absolutely flourishes as the audience's excitement and cheering builds to a Best in Show or Best in Trial finish.

tional. Even if his owner may be unfair or inconsiderate, the Kees continues to love with unflagging intensity.

The Keeshond is basically a very happy breed. In fact, there are those who say that the term "jump for joy" was coined just for this breed. You will find a Kees completely capable of jumping several feet straight up in the air from a complete standstill. This is all well and good, but might be intimidating for those who don't know that your treasured pet is simply telling the world how happy he is. It is best to teach your Kees puppy early on that jumping up on people is definitely something that must not be done.

Furthermore, the breed's jumping ability does not always respect such boundaries as fences—especially not when the fence stands between where a Kees is and where he feels he should be. The kennel run or yard in which your Keeshond lives can never be fenced too high, nor can it be too securely locked. These fellows are near-genius at undoing things!

Since the Keeshond has limited hunting or prey instinct, the breed is particularly gregarious and amiable. A Kees is an excellent candidate for the household in which children, other dogs and practically any other kind of pet might also live.

Should all these wonderful characteristics of the breed lead you to think the Keeshond is an exceptionally intelligent breed of dog, you are definitely on the right track. However, if the breed's intelligence causes you to think there will be little or no

---

TAKE A LICKIN'

Your Keeshond's attempts to lick your face are acknowledgment of your role as pack leader. This is behavior passed down through the ages from the Keeshond's wolf ancestors.

---

effort involved in transforming the fluffy little cherub you bring home into a well-behaved canine good citizen, think again!

The Keeshond has a mind of his own and at times will use every bit of that canine intelligence to work around any and all of those household rules that interfere with his having a good time. A well-trained Keeshond around the home is an absolute delight. The operative words here are, of course, "well-trained."

The untrained Kees is an absolute nuisance! The same intelligence that can produce a happy well-adjusted companion can also head off in an extremely negative direction. An untrained Kees can be exasperating. This is a high-energy, agile and quick-thinking breed, entirely capable of reducing your home to a shambles.

Dogs are not born with an ability to understand the concept of right and wrong. The Keeshond is no exception. Either a dog derives pleasure from an act or he does not. Approval, petting and being fussed over are

Due to their superior intelligence and trainability, Keeshonden excel at agility and obedience work. This Kees is jumping over an obstacle at an agility trial.

good. The only way your Kees will know what is bad and wrong is if you are constantly there reminding him that this is the case.

"SALTY DOG"

The Keeshond makes an ideal dog for boat owners. The breed has a natural affinity for living on a boat and becomes extremely protective of his surroundings. Many Kees, if given the opportunity of spending idle hours on land or aboard their owners' boats, will opt for the latter, and a Kees is always ready, willing and able to set off to discover parts unknown.

These reminders cannot be randomly enforced. A dog's mind cannot grasp the concept of "right sometimes and wrong others." This is confusing and bewildering to a breed with the intelligence level of the Keeshond. Your Kees is able to learn that he is wrong to lounge on the sofa, if in fact it is wrong and wrong all the time. Otherwise, it may easily become a case of wrong when you are there but perfectly OK when you are not. The most important lesson you will ever teach your Keeshond is that there are rules and there are no exceptions to them.

The breed standard not only describes the desirable physical and personality traits of the breed but also defines the proper movement for the breed. The judge will assess the Keeshond's movement by having the handler gait the dog in the ring.

INTRODUCTION TO THE STANDARD

In the earliest days of man's relationship with dogs, he began to see that those dogs constructed in a certain way were better suited to performing a particular task. Particular characteristics were prized so breeding practices were employed to perpetuate those characteristics. The people who kept these dogs gathered to make comparisons and seek out stock to improve their own lines. The more successful keepers were asked to observe the dogs at work and evaluate them.

With urbanization, fewer and fewer dogs were given the opportunity to perform their intended functions. To avoid the respective breeds' losing their ability to perform, dog fanciers began to select their stock on the basis of the conformation they determined would produce the most successful workers. The guidelines became theoretical rather than practical.

Previously the accent had been on function, now it was on form. It should be easy to see that, once form was the keynote, breeds whose only purpose was to be asthetically pleasing would gain an equal place of respect alongside their working relatives.

It should be noted here that these early descriptions were the forerunners of breed standards and that they were written by knowledgeable individuals in the breed for their peers. They were all thoroughly familiar with their breeds, and the descriptions were used primarily as checklists or blueprints to breed by, reminders so that important points of conformation would not be lost.

Today's standards describe the ideal specimen of a breed. They are written by individuals versed in breed type and canine anatomy. They include descriptions of structure, temperament, coat and color and gait, the manner in which the dog moves.

The standards are used by breeders to assist them in breeding toward this goal of perfection. While no dog is absolutely perfect, the dogs that adhere closest to the ideal are what breeders will determine is show or breeding stock, and the dogs that deviate to any great extent are considered companion or pet stock. In all cases, the dog's temperament and soundness are essential, whether a show dog, breeding animal or pet. Likewise, the standard is also used by dog show judges to compare actual dogs to the ideal. The dog adhering most closely to this ideal is the winner of the class.

AMERICAN KENNEL CLUB BREED STANDARD FOR THE KEESHOND

GENERAL APPEARANCE
The Keeshond (pronounced *kayz-hawnd*) is a natural, handsome dog of well-balanced, short-coupled body, attracting attention not only by his coloration, alert carriage, and intelligent expression, but also by his stand-off coat, his richly plumed tail well curled over his back, his foxlike expression, and his small pointed ears. His coat is very thick around the neck, fore part of the shoulders and chest, forming a lion-like ruff—more profuse in the male. His rump and hind legs, down to the hocks, are also thickly coated, forming the characteristic "trousers." His head, ears, and lower legs are covered with thick, short hair.

SIZE, PROPORTION, SUBSTANCE
The Keeshond is a medium-sized, square-appearing, sturdy dog, neither coarse nor lightly made. The ideal height of fully matured dogs when measured from top of withers to the ground is 18 inches for males and 17 inches for bitches; a 1-inch variance either way is acceptable. While correct size is very important, it should not outweigh that of type.

HEAD
Expression: Expression is largely dependent on the distinctive characteristic called "spectacles," a combination of markings and shadings in the orbital area which must include a delicate, dark line slanting from the outer corner of each eye toward the lower corner of each ear coupled with expressive eyebrows. Markings (or shadings) on face and head must present a pleasing appearance, imparting to the dog an alert and intelligent expression. Very *Serious Fault:* Absence of dark lines which form the "spectacles."

A correct Keeshond head, showing the desired spectacle markings around the eyes.

An ideal Keeshond of correct type, balance, coat and color pattern.

Eyes: Eyes should be dark brown in color, of medium size, almond shaped, set obliquely and neither too wide apart nor too close together. Eye rims are black. *Faults:* Round and/or protruding eyes or eyes light of color.

Ears: Ears should be small, triangular in shape, mounted high on head and carried erect. Size should be proportionate to the head-length approximating the distance from the outer corner of the eye to the nearest edge of the ear. *Fault:* Ears not carried erect when at attention.

Skull: The head should be well-proportioned to the body and wedge-shaped when viewed from above—not only the muzzle, but the whole head should give this impression when the ears are drawn back by covering the nape of the neck and the ears with one hand. Head in profile should exhibit a definite stop. *Faults:* Apple head or absence of stop.

Muzzle: Of medium length, neither coarse nor snipey, and well proportioned to the skull.

Mouth: The mouth should be neither overshot nor undershot. Lips should be black and closely meeting—not thick, coarse or sagging, and with no wrinkle at the corner of the mouth. *Faults:* Overshot, undershot or wry mouth.

Incorrect head, showing light eyes and lacking the characteristic spectacle markings around the eyes.

Incorrect head, showing ears too large and set too far apart; muzzle too long; coat lacking fullness, too flat with poor markings.

Teeth: The teeth should be white, sound and strong meeting in a scissors bite. Fault: Misaligned teeth.

Neck, Topline, Body

The neck should be moderately long, well-shaped and well set on shoulders. The body should be compact with a short, straight back sloping slightly downward toward the hindquarters: well ribbed, barrel well rounded, short in loin, belly moderately tucked up, deep and strong of chest.

Tail

The tail should be moderately long and well feathered, set on high and tightly curled over the back. It should lie flat and close to the body. The tail must form a part of the "silhouette" of the dog's body, rather than give the appearance of an appendage. *Fault:* Tail not lying close to the back.

Forequarters

Forelegs should be straight seen from any angle. Pasterns are strong with a slight slope. Legs must be of good bone in proportion to the overall dog. Shoulder to upper arm angulation is between slight to moderate.

Hindquarters

Angulation in rear should be between slight to moderate to complement the forequarters, creating balance and typical gait. Hindquarters are well muscled with hocks perpendicular to the ground.

Feet

The feet should be compact, well rounded, cat-like. Toes are nicely arched, with black nails.

Coat

The body should be abundantly covered with long, straight, harsh hair standing well out from a thick, downy undercoat. Head, including muzzle, skull and ears, should be covered with smooth, soft, short hair—velvety in texture on the ears. The neck is covered with a mane—more profuse in the male—sweeping from under the jaw and covering the whole of the front part of the shoulders and chest, as well as the top part of the shoulders. The hair on the legs should be smooth and short, except for feathering on the front legs and "trousers" on the hind legs. Hind legs should be

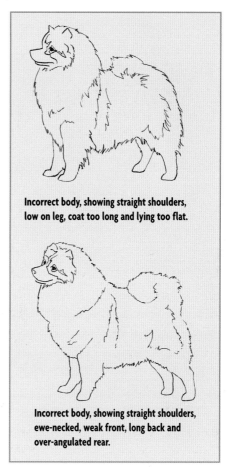

Incorrect body, showing straight shoulders, low on leg, coat too long and lying too flat.

Incorrect body, showing straight shoulders, ewe-necked, weak front, long back and over-angulated rear.

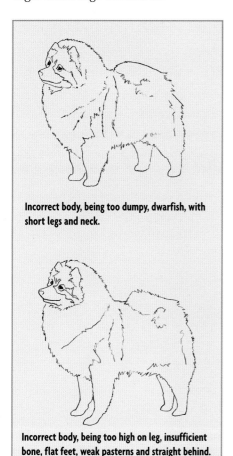

Incorrect body, being too dumpy, dwarfish, with short legs and neck.

Incorrect body, being too high on leg, insufficient bone, flat feet, weak pasterns and straight behind.

profusely feathered down to the hocks-not below. The hair on the tail should form a rich plume. Coat must not part down the back. The Keeshond is to be shown in a natural state with trimming permissible only on feet, pasterns, hocks and—if desired—whiskers. Trimming other than as described to be severely penalized. *Faults:* Silky, wavy, or curly coats. Part in coat down the back.

In Holland the Keeshond can have many colors. In the UK and US, it only can be any shade of gray. The dog shown above from Holland is solid white.

A solid black Keeshond from Holland.

COLOR AND MARKINGS
A dramatically marked dog, the Keeshond is a mixture of gray, black and cream. This coloration may vary from light to dark. The hair of the outer coat is black tipped, the length of the black tips producing the characteristic shading of color. Puppies are often less intensely marked. The undercoat is very pale gray or cream, never tawny.

Head: The muzzle should be dark in color. "Spectacles" and shadings, as previously described, are characteristic of the breed and must be present to some degree. Ears should be very dark-almost black.

Ruff, Shoulders and "Trousers": The color of the ruff and "trousers" is lighter than that of the body. The shoulder line markings of light gray must be well defined.

Tail: The plume of the tail is very light in color when curled on the back, and the tip of the tail should be black.

Legs and Feet: Legs and feet are cream.

Faults: Pronounced white markings. Black markings more than halfway down the foreleg, penciling excepted. White foot or feet.

MEETING THE IDEAL
The American Kennel Club defines a standard as: "A description of the ideal dog of each recognized breed, to serve as an ideal against which dogs are judged at shows." This "blueprint" is drawn up by the breed's recognized parent club, approved by a majority of its membership, and then submitted to the AKC for approval. This is a complete departure from the way standards are handled in England, where all standards and changes are controlled by The Kennel Club.

Very Serious Faults: Entirely black or white or any solid color; any pronounced deviation from the color as described.

GAIT
The distinctive gait of the Keeshond is unique to the breed. Dogs should move boldly and keep tails curled over the back. They should move cleanly and briskly; the movement should be straight and sharp with reach and drive between slight to moderate.

TEMPERAMENT
Temperament is of primary importance. The Keeshond is neither timid nor aggressive but, instead, is outgoing and friendly with both people and other dogs. The Keeshond is a lively, intelligent, alert and affectionate companion.

Approved November 14, 1989
Effective January 1, 1990

KEESHOND

SELECTING FROM THE LITTER

Before you visit a litter of puppies, promise yourself that you won't fall for the first pretty face you see! Decide on your goals for your puppy—show prospect, hunting dog, obedience competitor, family companion—and then look for a puppy who displays the appropriate qualities. In most litters, there is an Alpha pup (the bossy puppy), and occasionally a shy fellow who is less confident, with the rest of the litter falling somewhere in the middle. "Middle-of-the-roaders" are safe bets for most families and novice competitors.

THINGS TO CONSIDER

Visiting the home or kennel where there is a litter of puppies is probably not the best idea in the world if you haven't fully decided whether or not to add a Keeshond to your household. Chances are you will leave with a puppy—ready or not! Kees puppies are absolutely irresistible. There is positively nothing quite so captivating as these little bundles of fluff, and their little wind-up-toy antics can keep the onlooker fascinated for hours.

For this very reason, the person anticipating owning a Kees should give serious thought to the final decision. All puppies are cuddly and cute—Kees puppies particularly so, with their mischievous little expressions and perky attitudes. Nor is there anything more seductive than a litter of Keeshond puppies at play or nestled together sound asleep, piled one on top of the other. But in addition to being cute, Kees puppies are living, breathing and very mischievous little creatures. Not only that, they are totally dependent upon their human owners for all of their needs once they leave their mother and littermates.

CREATE A SCHEDULE

Puppies thrive on sameness and routine. Offer meals at the same time each day, take him out at regular times for potty trips and do the same for play periods and outdoor activity. Make note of when your puppy naps and when he is most lively and energetic, and try to plan his day around those times. Once he is house-trained and more predictable in his habits, he will be better able to tolerate changes in his schedule.

Buying a puppy, especially a soon to be very heavily coated dog, before someone is absolutely sure that he wants to make that commitment, can be a serious mistake. The prospective dog owner must clearly understand the amount of time and work involved in dog ownership. Failure to understand the extent of commitment that dog ownership involves is one of the primary reasons that there are so many unwanted canines that end their lives in animal shelters.

Before anyone contemplates the purchase of any dog, there are some very basic conditions that must be considered. One of the first important questions that must be answered is whether or not the person who will ultimately be responsible for the dog's day-to-day care and well-being actually wants a dog. Voluntarily or not, it all too often happens that one person in

the household becomes primarily responsible for the family dog's care. While the children in the family may be entirely enthusiastic about having a dog, it must be remembered they are away most of the day at school. Further, there are all those after-school activities that take up a good deal of a student's time. Then usually one of the parents must take on the additional responsibility of being the primary care-giver for the family pet. So the question that then must be answered is: does this person share the enthusiasm for taking on the additional responsibility?

Pets are a wonderful method of teaching responsibility to children, but keep in mind that the enthusiasm that inspires children to promise anything in order to have a new puppy may quickly wane. Who will take care of the puppy once the novelty wears off? Does that

Your puppy's life is in your hands. Are you ready to commit to the stewardship of a Keeshond's life?

SOME DAM ATTITUDE

When selecting a puppy, be certain to meet the dam of the litter. The temperament of the dam is often predictive of the temperament of her puppies. However, dams occasionally are very protective of their young, some to the point of being testy or aggressive with visitors, whom they may view as a danger to their babies. Such attitudes are more common when the pups are very young and still nursing and should not be mistaken for actual aggressive temperament. If possible, visit the dam away from her pups to make friends with her and gain a better understanding of her true personality.

person want a dog?

Furthermore, does the lifestyle of the family actually provide for responsible dog ownership? In this day and age, the entire family may be away from early morning to late at night. Who then will provide for all of a puppy's needs? Feeding, exercise, training, outdoor access and the like cannot be provided if no one is home.

HOW TO SELECT A BREEDER AND PUPPY

The purchase of any dog is an important step, since the well-cared-for dog will live with you for many years. In the case of a Keeshond, this could easily be 13 to 14 years, or even longer! You will undoubtedly want the dog you live with for that length of time to be one you will enjoy.

It is extremely important that a prospective Keeshond owner seek out an established breeder who has a long-standing record of producing mentally and physically sound dogs. Breeders with this experience know how important it is to use only those animals in their breeding programs that have proven their ability to produce healthy offspring with correct Keeshond temperament.

No breed is entirely exempt from producing an occasional maverick—an ill-tempered or physically unsound dog. However, the astute breeder eliminates animals of this kind from his breeding program, thus removing the possibility of having these undesirable traits passed on.

Early socialization is particularly important to the Keeshond if the potential for the breed's long-standing and reliable temperament is to be achieved. Puppies born and raised out in the garage or in a basement without regular human contact during the critical period between birth and 12 weeks of age are highly unlikely to develop the confidence necessary to be sound and reliable companions.

It is essential that your Kees is purchased from a breeder who has earned a reputation over the years for consistently producing dogs that are sound in both temperament and body. There are always those who are ready and willing to exploit a breed for financial gain with no

PET INSURANCE

Just as you can insure your car, your house and your own health, you likewise can insure your dog's health. Investigate a pet insurance policy by talking to your vet. Depending on the age of your dog, the breed and the kind of coverage you desire, your policy can be very affordable. Most policies cover accidental injuries, poisoning and thousands of medical problems and illnesses, including cancers. Some carriers also offer routine care and immunization coverage.

thought given to its health or welfare, or to the homes in which the dogs will be living.

The first question a prospective owner should ask a breeder is, "What is the number-one characteristic you breed for?" Deal only with those breeders who answer, "Good temperament." The responsible Kees breeder puts compatibility far ahead of any other characteristic. It will also tell the buyer which breeders actually live with their own dogs as pets—always a good sign.

The buyer should look for cleanliness in both the dogs and the areas in which the dogs are kept. Cleanliness is the first clue that tells you how much effort the breeder puts into caring for his dogs.

Sometimes a breeder will have more than one litter on the premises, enabling you to see pups at different ages and stages of development.

Above all, the Kees puppy you buy should be a happy, bouncy extrovert. The worst thing you could possibly do is buy a shy, sickly or extremely nervous puppy in hopes of rehabilitating it. This will only lead to heartbreak and countless veterinary bills.

A healthy little Kees puppy will be strong and sturdy to the touch, never bony or, on the other hand, obese and bloated. The

A soft, lustrous coat, sturdy construction and lovely temperament sum up the ideal Kees puppy.

PEDIGREE VS. REGISTRATION CERTIFICATE

Too often new owners are confused between these two important documents. Your puppy's pedigree, essentially a family tree, is a written record of a dog's genealogy of three generations or more. The pedigree will show you the names as well as performance titles of all dogs in your pup's background. Your breeder must provide you with a registration application, with his part properly filled out. You must complete the application and send it to the AKC with the proper fee. Every puppy must come from a litter that has been AKC-registered by the breeder, born in the US and from a sire and dam that are also registered with the AKC.

The seller must provide you with complete records to identify the puppy. The AKC requires that the seller provide the buyer with the following: breed; sex, color and markings; date of birth; litter number (when available); names and registration numbers of the parents; breeder's name; and date sold or delivered.

inside of the puppy's ears should be pink and clean. Dark discharge or a bad odor could indicate ear mites, a sure sign of poor maintenance. The healthy Kees puppy's breath smells sweet. The teeth are clean and white, and there should never be any malformation of the mouth or jaw. The puppy's eyes should be clear and bright. Eyes that appear runny and irritated indicate serious problems. There should be no sign of discharge from the nose, nor should it be crusted or runny. Coughing and diarrhea are danger signals, as are any eruptions on the skin. The coat should be soft and lustrous. The healthy Kees puppy's front legs should be straight as little posts and the movement light and bouncy. The best way to describe a Kees puppy's movement is like that of a mechanical wind-up toy with legs that cover considerable ground.

As careful as respected breeders are about the stock they use in their breeding programs and the early socialization they give their dogs, the new owner must assume his own responsibility in the socialization process. A Keeshond may be an absolutely delightful companion within the confines of his home, but if your dog never leaves its home or sees a stranger, the situation can be entirely different. Street noises and strangers can be terrifying to the dog who has had

no experience coping with these day-to-day experiences. Waiting until your Kees is an adult to start exposure to these events may delay or completely preclude the possibility of your dog's being able to ever handle these situations well. Socialization starts at the breeder's and continues from the moment you bring your new puppy home until all situations and people are taken in stride.

Puppies learn lots of important lessons from mom, including the official rules of play.

A SHOW PUPPY

If you plan to show your puppy, you must first deal with a reputable breeder who shows his dogs and has had some success in the conformation ring. The puppy's pedigree should include one or more champions in the first and second generation. You should be familiar with the breed and breed standard so you know what qualities to look for in your puppy. The breeder's observations and recommendations also are invaluable aids in selecting your future champion. If you consider an older puppy, be sure that the puppy has been properly socialized with people and not isolated in a kennel without substantial daily human contact.

A COMMITTED NEW OWNER

By now you should understand what makes the Keeshond a most unique and special dog, one that will fit nicely into your family and lifestyle. If you have researched breeders, you should be able to recognize a knowledgeable and responsible Keeshond breeder who cares not only about his pups but also about what kind of owner you will be. If you have completed the final step in your new journey, you have found a litter, or possibly two, of quality Keeshond pups.

A visit with the puppies and their breeder should be an education in itself. Breed research, breeder selection and puppy visitation are very important aspects of finding the puppy of your dreams. Beyond that, these things also lay the foundation for a successful future with your pup. Puppy personalities within each litter vary, from the shy and easygoing puppy to the one who is dominant and assertive, with most pups falling

somewhere in between. By spending time with the puppies you will be able to recognize certain behaviors and what these behaviors indicate about each pup's temperament. Which type of pup will complement your family dynamics is best determined by observing the puppies in action within their "pack." Your breeder's expertise and recommendations are also valuable. Although you may fall in love with a bold and brassy male, the breeder may suggest that another pup would be best for you. The breeder's experience in rearing Keeshond pups and matching their temperaments with appropriate humans offers the best assurance that your pup will meet your needs and expectations. The type of puppy that you select is just as important as your decision that the Keeshond is the breed for you.

The decision to live with a Keeshond is a serious commitment and not one to be taken lightly. This puppy is a living sentient

FIRST CAR RIDE

The ride to your home from the breeder will no doubt be your puppy's first automobile experience, and you should make every effort to keep him comfortable and secure. Bring a large towel or small blanket for the puppy to lie on during the trip, and an extra towel in case the pup gets carsick or has a potty accident. It's best to have another person with you to hold the puppy in his lap. Most puppies will fall fast asleep from the rolling motion of the car. If the ride is lengthy, your may have to stop so that the puppy can relieve himself, so be sure to bring a leash and collar for those stops. Avoid rest areas for potty trips, since they are frequented by many dogs, who may carry parasites or disease. It's better to stop at grassy areas near gas stations or shopping centers to prevent unhealthy exposure for your pup.

Take advantage of the opportunity to meet the dam of your chosen litter. The personality, activity level and temperament of the dam will indicate the likely traits of your puppy.

CREATE A SCHEDULE

Your puppy thrives on sameness and routine. Offer meals at the same time each day, take him out at regular times for potty trips and do the same for play periods and outdoor activity. Make note of when your puppy naps and when he is most lively and energetic, and try to plan his day around those times. Once he is house-trained and more predictable in his habits, he will be better able to tolerate changes in his schedule.

being that will be dependent on you for basic survival for his entire life. Beyond the basics of survival—food, water, shelter and protection—he needs much, much more. The new pup needs love, nurturing and a proper canine education to mold him into a responsible, well-behaved canine citizen. Your Keeshond's health and good manners will need consistent monitoring and regular "tune-ups." So your job as a responsible dog owner will be ongoing throughout every stage of his life. If you are not prepared to accept these responsibilities and commit to them for the next decade, likely longer, then you are not prepared to own a dog of any breed.

Although the responsibilities of owning a dog may at times tax your patience, the joy of living with your Keeshond far outweighs the workload, and a well-mannered adult dog is worth your time and effort. Before your very eyes, your new charge will grow up to be your most loyal friend, devoted to you unconditionally.

YOUR KEESHOND SHOPPING LIST

Just as expectant parents prepare a nursery for their baby, so should you ready your home for the arrival of your Keeshond pup. If you have the necessary puppy supplies purchased and in place before he comes home, it will ease the puppy's transition from the warmth

MAKE A COMMITMENT

Dogs are most assuredly man's best friend, but they are also a lot of work. When you add a puppy to your family, you also are adding to your daily responsibilities for the next 10 to 15 years. Dogs need more than just food, water and a place to sleep. They also require training (which can be ongoing throughout the lifetime of the dog), activity to keep them physically and mentally fit and hands-on attention every day, plus grooming and health care. Your life as you now know it may well disappear! Are you prepared for such drastic changes?

and familiarity of his mom and littermates to the brand-new environment of his new home and human family. You will be too busy to stock up and prepare your house after your pup comes home, that's for sure! Imagine how a pup must feel upon being transported to a strange new place. It's up to you to comfort him and to let your little pup know that he is going to be happy with you!

FOOD AND WATER BOWLS

Your puppy will need separate bowls for his food and water. Stainless steel pans are generally preferred over plastic bowls since they sterilize better and pups are less inclined to chew on the metal. Heavy-duty ceramic bowls are popular, but consider how often you will have to pick up those heavy bowls! Buy adult-sized pans, as your puppy will grow into them before you know it.

THE DOG CRATE

If you think that crates are tools of punishment and confinement for when a dog has misbehaved, think again. Most breeders and almost all trainers recommend a crate as the preferred house-training aid as well as for all-around puppy training and safety. Because dogs are natural den creatures that prefer cave-like environments, the benefits of crate use are many. The crate provides the puppy with his very own "safe house," a cozy place to sleep, take a break or seek comfort with a favorite toy; a travel aid to house

When you find the Keeshond puppy of your dreams, you will know it. The right pup will sparkle with personality, good health and soundness, characteristics that every dog owner rightly cherishes.

your dog when on the road, at motels or at the vet's office; a training aid to help teach your puppy proper toileting habits; a place of solitude when non-dog people happen to drop by and don't want a lively puppy—or even a well-behaved adult dog—saying hello or begging for attention.

Crates come in several types, although the wire crate and the fiberglass airline-type crate are the most popular. Both are safe and your puppy will adjust to either one, so the choice is up to you. The wire crates offer better visibility for the pup as well as better ventilation. Many of the wire crates easily collapse into suitcase-size carriers. The fiberglass crates, similar to those used by the airlines for animal transport, are sturdier and

Pet shops sell three crate styles: fiberglass, wire and plastic mesh. For the home, the wire crate is best for a Keeshond.

more den-like. However, the fiberglass crates do not collapse and are less ventilated than a wire crate, which can be problematic in hot weather. Some of the newer crates are made of heavy plastic mesh; they are very lightweight and fold up into slim-line suitcases. However, a mesh crate might not be suitable for a pup with manic chewing habits.

Don't bother with a puppy-sized crate. Although your Keeshond will be a wee fellow when you bring him home, he will grow up in the blink of an eye and your puppy crate will be useless. Purchase a crate that will accommodate an adult Keeshond. He will stand well over a foot tall when full grown, so a medium- to large-sized crate will fit him nicely.

BEDDING AND CRATE PADS

Your puppy will enjoy some type of soft bedding in his "room" (the crate), something he can snuggle into to feel cozy and secure. Old towels or blankets are good choices for a young pup, since he may (and probably will) have a toileting accident or two in the crate or decide to chew on the bedding material. Once he is fully trained and out of the early chewing stage, you can replace the puppy bedding with a permanent crate pad if you prefer. Crate pads and other dog beds run the gamut from inexpensive to high-end doggie-designer styles, but don't splurge on the good stuff until you are sure that your puppy is reliable and won't tear it up or make a mess on it.

PUPPY TOYS

Just as infants and older children require objects to stimulate their minds and bodies, puppies need toys to entertain their curious brains, wiggly paws and achy teeth. An array of safe doggie toys will help satisfy your puppy's chewing instincts and distract him from gnawing on the leg of your antique chair or your new leather sofa. Most puppy toys are cute and look like they would be a lot of fun, but not all are necessarily safe or good for your puppy so use caution when you go puppy-toy shopping.

Although Keeshonds are not known to be voracious chewers like many other dogs, they still love to chew. The best "chewcifiers" are nylon and hard rubber bones, which are safe to gnaw on and come in sizes appropriate for all age groups and breeds. Be especially careful of natural bones, which can splinter or develop dangerous sharp edges; pups can easily swallow or choke on those bone splinters. Veterinarians often tell of surgical nightmares involving bits of splintered bone, because in addition to the danger of choking, the sharp pieces can damage the intestinal tract.

Similarly, rawhide chews, while a favorite of most dogs and puppies, can be equally dangerous. Pieces of rawhide are easily swallowed after they get all gummy from chewing, and dogs have been known to choke on large pieces of ingested rawhide. Rawhide chews

ROCK-A-BYE BEDDING

The wide assortment of dog beds today can make your choice quite difficult, as there are many adorable novelty beds in fun styles and prints. It's wise to wait until your puppy has outgrown the chewing stage before providing him with a dog bed, since he might make confetti out of it. Your puppy will be happy with an old towel or blanket in his crate until he is old enough to resist the temptation to chew up his bed. For a dog of any age, a bed with a washable cover is always a wise choice.

TOYS 'R SAFE

The vast array of tantalizing puppy toys is staggering. Stroll through any pet shop or pet-supply outlet and you will see that the choices can be overwhelming. However, not all dog toys are safe or sensible. Most very young puppies enjoy soft woolly toys that they can snuggle with and carry around. (You know they have outgrown them when they shred them up!) Avoid toys that have buttons, tabs or other enhancements that can be chewed off and swallowed. Soft toys that squeak are fun, but make sure your puppy does not disembowel the toy and remove (and swallow) the squeaker. Toys that rattle or make noise can excite a puppy, but they present the same danger as the squeaky kind and thus require supervision. Hard rubber toys that bounce can also entertain a pup, but make sure that the toy is too big to be swallowed.

should be offered only when you can supervise the puppy.

Soft woolly toys are special puppy favorites. They come in a wide variety of cute shapes and sizes; some look like little stuffed animals. Puppies love to shake them up and toss them about, or simply carry them around. Be careful of fuzzy toys that have button eyes or noses that your pup could chew off and swallow, and make sure that he does not "disembowel" a squeaky toy to remove the squeaker! Braided rope toys are similar in that they are fun to chew and toss around, but they shred easily and the strings are easy to swallow. The strings are not digestible and, if the puppy doesn't pass them in his stool, he could end up at the vet's office. As with rawhides, your puppy should be closely monitored with rope toys.

If you believe that your pup has ingested one of these forbidden objects, check his stools for the next couple of days to see if he passes them when he defecates. At the same time, also watch for signs of intestinal distress. A call to your veterinarian might be in order to get his advice and be on the safe side.

An all-time favorite toy for puppies (young and old!) is the empty gallon milk jug. Hard plastic juice containers—46 ounces or more —are also excellent. Such containers make lots of noise when they are batted about and puppies go crazy with delight as they play with them. However, they don't often last very long, so be sure to remove and replace them when they get chewed up on the ends.

A word of caution about home-made toys: be careful with your choices of non-traditional play objects. Never use old shoes or socks, since a puppy cannot distinguish between the old ones on which he's allowed to chew and the new ones in your closet that are strictly off limits. That principle applies to anything that resembles something that you don't want your puppy to chew up.

COLLARS

A lightweight nylon collar is the best choice for a very young pup. Quick-clip collars are easy to put on and remove, and they can be adjusted as the puppy grows. Introduce him to his collar as soon as he comes home to get him accustomed to wearing it. He'll get used to it quickly and won't mind a bit. Make sure that it is snug enough that it won't slip off, yet loose enough to be comfortable for the pup. You should be able to slip two fingers between the collar and his neck. Check the collar often, as puppies grow in spurts and his collar can become too tight almost overnight. Choke collars are for training purposes only and should never be used on a puppy under four or five months old.

Choose a woven cotton or nylon collar for your Keeshond puppy. Be certain the collar fits securely, but not too snugly. The Keeshond's coat around the neck is abundant and will affect the tightness of the collar.

LEASHES

A 6-foot nylon lead is an excellent choice for a young puppy. It is lightweight and not as tempting to chew as a leather lead. You can switch to a 6-foot leather lead after your pup has grown and is used to

Breeders introduce the Keeshond pups to chew toys and crates during the critical development stages. A puppy purchased from a good breeder will have already had these valuable experiences.

COLLARING OUR CANINES

The standard flat collar with a buckle or a snap, in leather, nylon or cotton, is widely regarded as the everyday all-purpose collar. If the collar fits correctly, you should be able to fit two fingers between the collar and the dog's neck. The martingale, greyhound or limited-slip collar is preferred by many dog owners and trainers.

Leather Buckle Collars

Limited-Slip Collar

It is fixed with an extra loop that tightens when pressure is applied to the leash. The martingale collar gets tighter but does not "choke" the dog. The limited-slip collar should only be used for walking and training, not for free play or interaction with another dog. These types of collar should never be left on the dog, as the extra loop can lead to accidents.

Choke collars, usually made of stainless steel, are made for training purposes, though are not recommended for small dogs or heavily coated breeds. The chains can injure small dogs or damage long/abundant coats. Thin nylon choke leads are commonly used on show dogs while in the ring, though they are not practical for everyday use.

The harness, with two or three straps that attach over the dog's shoulders and around his torso, is a humane and safe alternative to the conventional collar. By and large, a well-made harness is virtually escape-proof. Harnesses are available in nylon and mesh and can be outfitted on most dogs, ranging from chest girths of 10 to 30 inches.

Snap Bolt Choke Collar

Harness

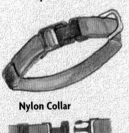

Nylon Collar

Quick-Click Closure

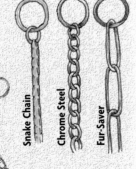

Snake Chain

Chrome Steel

Fur-Saver

Choke Chain Collars

A head collar, composed of a nylon strap that goes around the dog's muzzle and a second strap that wraps around his neck, offers the owner better control over his dog. This device is recommended for problem-solving with dogs (including jumping up, pulling and aggressive behaviors), but must be used with care.

A training halter, including a flat collar and two straps, made of nylon and webbing, is designed for walking. There are several on the market; some are more difficult to put on the dog than others. The halter harness, with two small slip rings at each end, is recommended for ease of use.

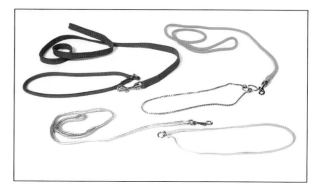

EASY, COWBOY!

Who's going to convince your dog that his rawhide toy isn't food? Dogs love rawhide and usually masticate the hide until it's soft enough to swallow. This can lead to choking or intestinal blockage, which is thankfully not terribly common. Another possible danger of rawhide results from the hides used in certain countries. Foreign hides can contain arsenic, lead, antibiotics or *Salmonella bacilli*. Even though imported chews are usually cheaper than American-made chews, this is one example in which buying American really counts.

Owners must carefully observe their dogs when they are chewing rawhide and remove any soft pieces that the dog pulls from the hide. Despite these drawbacks, rawhide chews do offer some benefits. Chewing rawhide can help keep the dog's teeth clean and distract your dog from chewing on your favorite leather loafers or sofa.

Once the puppy is heel trained with a traditional leash, you can consider purchasing a retractable lead. A flexible lead is excellent for walking adult dogs that are already leash-wise. The "flexi" allows the dog to roam farther away from you and explore a wider area when out walking, and also retracts when you need to keep him close to you.

When selecting items, like a lead and collar, that you will use every day, purchase the best quality that you can. Durable safe products will last longer and benefit both you and your dog.

Safe nylon and rubber toys are the best choices for the growing Kees's mouth.

walking politely on a lead. For initial puppy walks and house-training purposes, you should invest in a shorter lead so that you have more control over the puppy. At first, you don't want him wandering too far away from you, and when taking him out for toileting you will want to keep him in the specific area chosen for his potty spot.

HOME SAFETY FOR YOUR PUPPY

The importance of puppy-proofing cannot be overstated. In addition to making your house comfortable for your Keeshond's arrival, you also must make sure that your house is safe for your puppy before you bring him home. There are countless hazards in the owner's personal living environment that a pup can sniff, chew, swallow or destroy. Many are obvious; others are not. Do a thorough advance house check to remove or rearrange those things that could hurt your puppy, keeping any potentially dangerous items out of areas to which he will have access.

Electrical cords are especially dangerous, since puppies view them as irresistible chew toys. Unplug and remove all exposed cords or fasten them beneath a baseboard where the puppy cannot reach them. Veterinarians and fire-fighters can tell you horror stories about electrical burns and house fires that resulted from puppy-chewed electrical cords. Consider this a most serious precaution for your puppy and the rest of your family.

Scout your home for tiny objects that might be seen at a pup's eye level. Keep medication bottles and cleaning supplies well out of reach, and do the same with waste baskets and other trash containers. It goes without saying that you should not use rodent poison or other toxic chemicals in any puppy area and that you must keep such containers safely locked up. You will be amazed at how many places a curious puppy can discover!

THE GRASS IS ALWAYS GREENER

Must dog owners decide between their beloved canine pals and their perfectly manicured emerald-green lawns? Just as dog urine is no tonic for growing grass, lawn chemicals are extremely dangerous to your dog. Fertilizers, pesticides and herbicides pose real threats to canines and humans alike. Dogs should be kept off treated grounds for at least 24 hours following treatment. Consider some organic options for your lawn care: use a homemade compost or a natural fertilizer instead of a commercial chemical. Some dog-conscious lawnkeepers avoid fertilizers entirely, keeping up their lawns by watering, aerating, mowing and seeding frequently.

As always, dogs complicate the equation. Canines love grass. They roll in it, eat it and love to bury their noses in it—and then do their business in it! Grass can mean hours of feel-good, smell-good fun! In addition to the dangers of lawn-care chemicals, there's also the threat of burs, thorns and pebbles in the grass, not to mention the very common grass allergy. Many dogs develop an incurably itchy skin condition from grass, especially in the late summer when the world is in full bloom.

LEASH LIFE

Dogs love leashes! Believe it or not, most dogs dance for joy every time their owners pick up their leashes. The leash means that the dog is going for a walk—and there are few things more exciting than that! Here are some of the kinds of leashes that are commercially available.

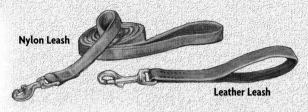

Nylon Leash

Leather Leash

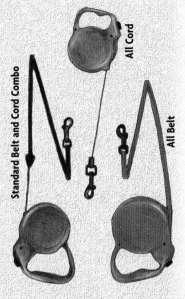

Standard Belt and Cord Combo

All Cord

All Belt

Retractable Leashes

Traditional Leash: Made of cotton, nylon or leather, these leashes are usually about 6 feet in length. A quality-made leather leash is softer on the hands than a nylon one. Durable woven cotton is a popular option. Lengths can vary up to about 48 feet, designed for different uses.

Chain Leash: Usually a metal chain leash with a plastic handle. This is not the best choice for most breeds, as it is heavier than other leashes and difficult to manage.

Retractable Leash: A long nylon cord is housed in a plastic device for extending and retracting. This leash, also known as a flexible leash, is ideal for taking trained dogs for long walks in open areas, although it is not recommended for large, powerful breeds. Different lengths and sizes are available, so check that you purchase one appropriate for your dog's weight.

Elastic Leash: A nylon leash with an elastic extension. This is useful for well-trained dogs, especially in conjunction with a head halter.

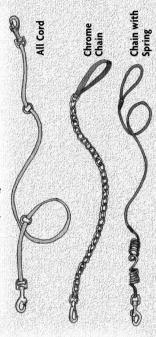

All Cord

Chrome Chain

Chain with Spring

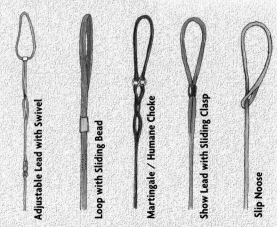

Adjustable Lead with Swivel

Loop with Sliding Bead

Martingale / Humane Choke

Show Lead with Sliding Clasp

Slip Noose

A Variety of Collar-Leash-in-One Products

Avoid leashes that are completely elastic, as they afford minimal control to the handler.

Adjustable Leash: This has two snaps, one on each end, and several metal rings. It is handy if you need to tether your dog temporarily, but is never to be used with a choke collar.

Tab Leash: A short leash (4 to 6 inches long) that attaches to your dog's collar. This device serves like a handle, in case you have to grab your dog while he's exercising off lead. It's ideal for "half-trained" dogs or dogs that only listen half the time.

Slip Leash: Essentially a leash with a collar built in, similar to what a dog-show handler uses to show a dog. This British-style collar has a ring on the end so that you can form a slip collar. Useful if you have to catch your own runaway dog or a stray.

A Dog-Safe Home

The dog-safety police are taking you and your new puppy on a house tour. Let's go room by room and see how safe your own home is for your new pup. The following items are doggie dangers, so either they must be removed or the dog should be monitored or not have access to these areas.

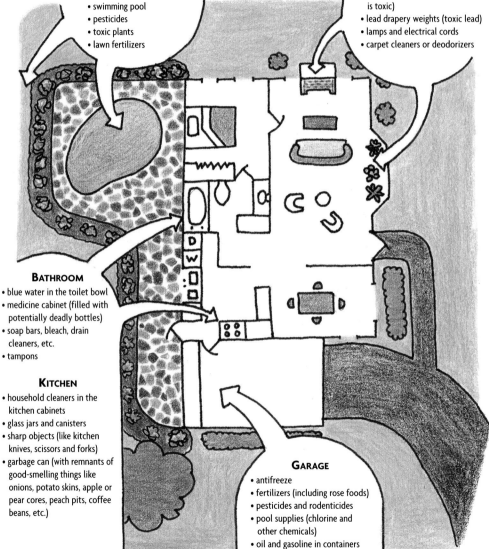

Living Room
- house plants (some varieties are poisonous)
- fireplace or wood-burning stove
- paint on the walls (lead-based paint is toxic)
- lead drapery weights (toxic lead)
- lamps and electrical cords
- carpet cleaners or deodorizers

Outdoor
- swimming pool
- pesticides
- toxic plants
- lawn fertilizers

Bathroom
- blue water in the toilet bowl
- medicine cabinet (filled with potentially deadly bottles)
- soap bars, bleach, drain cleaners, etc.
- tampons

Kitchen
- household cleaners in the kitchen cabinets
- glass jars and canisters
- sharp objects (like kitchen knives, scissors and forks)
- garbage can (with remnants of good-smelling things like onions, potato skins, apple or pear cores, peach pits, coffee beans, etc.)

Garage
- antifreeze
- fertilizers (including rose foods)
- pesticides and rodenticides
- pool supplies (chlorine and other chemicals)
- oil and gasoline in containers
- sharp objects, electrical cords and power tools

Once your house has cleared inspection, check your yard. A sturdy fence, well embedded into the ground, will give your dog a safe place to play and potty. Although Keeshonds are not known to be climbers or fence jumpers, they are still athletic dogs, so a 5- to 6-foot-high fence should be adequate to contain an agile youngster or adult. Check the fence periodically for necessary repairs. If there is a weak link or space to squeeze through, you can be sure a determined

Keeshond will discover it.

The garage and shed can be hazardous places for a pup, as things like fertilizers, chemicals and tools are usually kept there. It's best to keep these areas off limits to the pup. Antifreeze is especially dangerous to dogs, as they find the taste appealing and it takes only a few licks from the driveway to kill a dog, puppy or adult, small breed or large.

Never compromise when choosing your Kees's vet. You need a person who can communicate with you and with whom you feel comfortable. Your dog's health depends on a good relationship with your vet.

ARE VACCINATIONS NECESSARY?

Vaccinations are recommended for all puppies by the American Veterinary Medical Association (AVMA). Some vaccines are absolutely necessary, while others depend upon a dog's or puppy's individual exposure to certain diseases or the animal's immune history. According to the law, rabies vaccinations are required in all 50 states. Some diseases are fatal while others are treatable, making the need for vaccinating against the latter questionable. Follow your veterinarian's recommendations to keep your dog fully immunized and protected. You can also review the AVMA directive on vaccinations on their website: www.avma.org.

VISITING THE VETERINARIAN

A good veterinarian is your Keeshond puppy's best health insurance policy. If you do not already have a vet, ask friends and experienced dog people in your area for recommendations so that you can select a vet before you bring your Keeshond puppy home. Also arrange for your puppy's first veterinary examination beforehand, since many vets have two- and three-week waiting periods, and your puppy should visit the vet within a day or so of coming home.

It's important to make sure your puppy's first visit to the vet is a pleasant and positive one. The vet should take great care to befriend the pup and handle him gently to make their first meeting a positive experience. The vet will give the pup a thorough physical examination and set up a schedule for vaccinations and other necessary wellness visits. Be sure to show your vet any health and inoculation records, which you should have received from your breeder. Your vet is a great source of canine health information, so be sure to ask questions and take notes. Creating a health journal for your puppy will make a handy reference for his wellness and any future health problems that may arise.

MEETING THE FAMILY

Your Keeshond's homecoming is an exciting time for all members of the family, and it's only natural that everyone will be eager to meet him, pet him and play with him. However, for the puppy's sake, it's best to make these initial family meetings as uneventful as possible so that the pup is not overwhelmed with too much too soon. Remember, he has just left his dam and his littermates and is away from the breeder's home for the first time. Despite his fuzzy wagging tail, he is still apprehensive and wondering where he is and who all these strange humans are. It's best

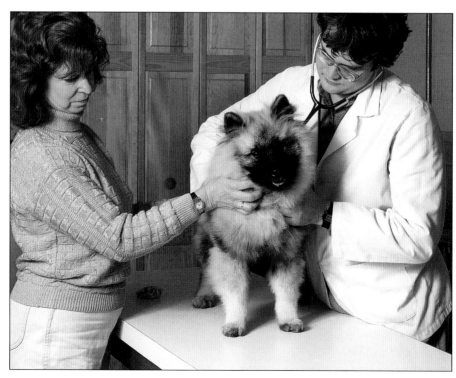

You should have your new Keeshond puppy examined by the vet soon after brining him home.

to let him explore on his own and meet the family members as he feels comfortable. Let him investigate all the new smells, sights and sounds at his own pace. Children should be especially careful to not get overly excited, use loud voices or hug the pup too tightly. Be calm, gentle and affectionate, and be ready to comfort him if he appears frightened or uneasy.

Be sure to show your puppy his new crate during this first day home. Toss a treat or two inside the crate; if he associates the crate with food, he will associate the crate with good things. If he is comfortable with the crate, you can offer him his first meal inside it. Leave the door ajar so he can wander in and out as he chooses.

FIRST NIGHT IN HIS NEW HOME

So much has happened in your Keeshond puppy's first day away from the breeder. He's had his first car ride to his new home. He's met his new human family and perhaps the other family pets. He has explored his new house and yard,

at least those places where he is to be allowed during his first weeks at home. He may have visited his new veterinarian. He has eaten his first meal or two away from his dam and littermates. Surely that's enough to tire out an eight-week-old Keeshond pup...or so you hope!

It's bedtime. During the day, the pup investigated his crate, which is his new den and sleeping space, so it is not entirely strange to him. Line the crate with a soft towel or blanket that he can snuggle into and gently place him into the crate for the night. Some breeders send home a piece of bedding from where the pup slept with his littermates, and those familiar scents are

The grass feels and smells so good—who would suspect so many dangers lurking in those emerald blades?

PUPPY PARASITES

Parasites are nasty little critters that live in or on your dog or puppy. Most puppies are born with ascarid roundworms, which are acquired from dormant roundworms residing in the dam. Other parasites can be acquired through contact with infected fecal matter. Take a stool sample to your vet for testing. He will prescribe a safe wormer to treat any parasites found in your puppy's stool. Always have a fecal test performed at your puppy's annual veterinary exam.

a great comfort for the puppy on his first night without his siblings.

He will probably whine or cry. The puppy is objecting to the confinement and the fact that he is alone for the first time. This can be a stressful time for you as well as for the pup. It's important that you remain strong and don't let the puppy out of his crate to comfort him. He will fall asleep eventually. If you release him, the puppy will learn that crying means "out" and will continue that habit. You are laying the groundwork for future habits. Some breeders find that soft music can soothe a crying pup and help him get to sleep.

SOCIALIZING YOUR PUPPY

The next 20 weeks of your Keeshond puppy's life are the most important of his entire lifetime. A properly socialized puppy will grow up to be a confident and stable adult who will be a pleasure to live with and a welcome addition to the neighborhood.

The importance of socialization cannot be overemphasized. Research on canine behavior has proven that puppies who are not exposed to new sights, sounds, people and animals during their first 20 weeks of life will grow up to be timid and fearful, even aggressive, and unable to flourish outside of their home environment

Socializing your puppy is not difficult and, in fact, will be a fun time for you both. Lead training goes hand in hand with socialization, so your puppy will be learning how to walk on a lead at the same time that he's meeting the neighborhood. Because the Keeshond is such a terrific breed, your puppy will enjoy being "the new kid on the block." Take him for short walks, to the park and to other dog-friendly places where he will encounter new people, especially children. Puppies automatically recognize children as "little people" and are drawn to play with them. Just make sure that you supervise these meetings and that the children do not get too rough or encourage him to play too hard. An overzealous pup can often nip too hard, frightening the child and in turn making the puppy overly excited. A bad experience in

Make your Keeshond's new home environment friendly and safe for him from the moment he arrives.

THE CRITICAL SOCIALIZATION PERIOD

Canine research has shown that a puppy's 8th through 16th week is the most critical learning period of his life. This is when the puppy "learns to learn," a time when he needs positive experiences to build confidence and stability. Puppies who are not exposed to different people and situations outside the home during this period can grow up to be fearful and sometimes aggressive. This is also the best time for puppy lessons, since he has not yet acquired any bad habits that could undermine his ability to learn.

puppyhood can impact a dog for life, so a pup that has a negative experience with a child may grow up to be shy or even aggressive around children.

Take your puppy along on your daily errands. Puppies are natural "people magnets," and most people who see your pup will want to pet him. All of these encounters will help to mold him into a confident adult dog. Likewise, you will soon feel like a confident, responsible dog owner, rightly proud of your handsome Keeshond.

Be especially careful of your puppy's encounters and experiences during the eight-to-ten-week-old period, which is also called the "fear period." This is a serious imprinting period, and all contact during this time should be gentle and positive. A frightening or negative event could leave a permanent impression that could affect his future behavior if a similar situation arises.

Also make sure that your puppy has received his first and second rounds of vaccinations before you expose him to other dogs or bring him to places that other dogs may frequent. Avoid dog parks and other strange-dog areas until your vet assures you that your puppy is fully immunized and resistant to the diseases that can be passed between canines. Discuss socialization with your breeder, as some breeders recommend socializing the puppy even before he has received all his inoculations, depending on how outgoing the puppy may be.

LEADER OF THE PUPPY'S PACK

Like other canines, your puppy needs an authority figure, someone he can look up to and regard as the leader of his "pack." His first pack leader was his dam, who taught him to be polite and not chew too hard on her ears or nip at her muzzle. He learned those same lessons from his littermates. If he played too rough, they cried in pain and stopped the game, which sent an important message to the rowdy puppy.

As puppies play together, they

are also struggling to determine who will be the boss. Being pack animals, dogs need someone to be in charge. If a litter of puppies remained together beyond puppy-hood, one of the pups would emerge as the strongest one, the one who calls the shots.

Once your puppy leaves the pack, he will look intuitively for a new leader. If he does not recognize you as that leader, he will try to assume that position for himself. Of course, it is hard to imagine your adorable Keeshond puppy trying to be in charge when he is so small and seemingly helpless. You must remember that these are natural canine instincts. Do not cave in and allow your pup to get the upper "paw"!

Just as socialization is so important during these first 20

weeks, so too is your puppy's early education. He was born without any bad habits. He does not know what is good or bad behavior. If he does things like nipping and digging, it's because he is having fun and doesn't know that humans consider these things as "bad." It's your job to teach him proper puppy manners, and this is the best time to accomplish that...before he has developed bad habits, since it is much more difficult to "unlearn" or correct unacceptable learned behavior than to teach good behavior from the start.

Make sure that all members of the family understand the importance of being consistent when training their new puppy. If you tell the puppy to stay off the sofa, and your daughter allows him to cuddle on the couch to watch her favorite television show, your pup will be confused about what he is and is not allowed to do. Have a family conference before your pup comes home so that everyone understands the basic principles of puppy training and the rules you have set forth for the pup, and agrees to follow them.

The old adage that "an ounce of prevention is worth a pound of cure" is especially true when it comes to puppies. It is much easier to prevent inappropriate behavior than it is to change it. It's also easier and less stressful for the pup, since it will keep discipline to a minimum and create a more posi-

MEET AND MINGLE

Puppies need to meet people and see the world if they are to grow up confident and unafraid. Take your puppy with you on everyday outings and errands. On-lead walks around the neighborhood and to the park offer the pup good exposure to the goings-on of his new human world. Avoid areas frequented by other dogs until your puppy has had his full round of puppy shots; ask your vet when your pup will be properly protected. Arrange for your puppy to meet new people of all ages every week.

THE FAMILY FELINE

A resident cat has feline squatter's rights. The cat will treat the newcomer (your puppy) as he sees fit, regardless of what you do or say. So it's best to let the two of them work things out on their own terms. Cats have a height advantage and will generally leap to higher ground to avoid direct contact with a rambunctious pup. Some will hiss and boldly swat at a pup who passes by or tries to reach the cat. Keep the puppy under control in the presence of the cat and they will eventually become accustomed to each other.

Here's a hint: move the cat's litter box where the puppy can't get into it! It's best to do so well before the pup comes home so the cat is used to the new location.

into mischief. If he starts to chew the corner of the rug, you can distract him instantly by tossing a toy for him to fetch. You also will be able to whisk him outside when you notice that he is about to piddle on the carpet. If you can't see your puppy, you can't teach or correct his behavior.

SOLVING PUPPY PROBLEMS

CHEWING AND NIPPING

Nipping at fingers and toes is normal puppy behavior. Chewing is also the way that puppies investigate their surroundings. However, you will have to teach your puppy that chewing anything other than his toys is not acceptable. That won't happen overnight and, at times, puppy teeth will test your

tive learning environment for him. That, in turn, will also be easier on you!

Here are a few common sense tips to keep your belongings safe and your puppy out of trouble:

- Keep your closet doors closed and your shoes, socks and other apparel off the floor so your puppy can't get at them.
- Keep a secure lid on the trash container or put the trash where your puppy can't dig into it. He can't damage what he can't reach!
- Supervise your puppy at all times to make sure he is not getting

Consistent house rules must be established once your Keeshond comes home. Without rules and a leader, your house will be overrun by unruly canines.

patience. However, if you allow nipping and chewing to continue, just think about the damage that a mature Keeshond can do with a full set of adult teeth.

Whenever your puppy nips your hand or fingers, cry out "Ouch!" in a loud voice, which should startle your puppy and stop him from nipping, even if only for a moment. Immediately distract him by offering a small treat or an appropriate toy for him to chew instead (which means having chew toys and puppy treats handy or in your pockets at all times). Praise him when he takes the toy and tell him what a good fellow he is. Praise is just as, or even more, important to puppy training as discipline and correction.

Puppies also tend to nip at children more often than adults, since they perceive little ones to be more vulnerable and more similar to their littermates. Teach your children appropriate responses to nipping behavior and, if they are unable to handle it themselves, you may have to intervene. Puppy nips can be quite painful, and a child's frightened reaction will only encourage a puppy to nip harder, which is a natural canine response. As with all other puppy situations, interaction between your Keeshond puppy and children should be supervised.

Chewing on objects, not just family members' fingers and ankles, is also normal canine behavior that can be especially tedious (for the owner, not the pup) during the teething period when the puppy's adult teeth are coming in. At this stage, chewing just plain feels good. Furniture legs and cabinet corners are common puppy favorites. Shoes and other personal items also taste pretty good to a pup.

The best solution is, once again, prevention. If you value something, keep it tucked away and out of reach. You can't hide your dining-room table in a closet, but you can try to deflect the chewing by applying a bitter product made just to deter dogs from chewing. Available in a spray or cream, this substance is vile-tasting, although safe for dogs, and most puppies will avoid the forbidden object after one tiny taste. You also can apply the product to your leather leash if the puppy tries to chew on his lead during leash-training sessions.

JUMPING UP

Although Keeshond pups are not known to be notorious jumpers, they are still puppies after all, and puppies jump up...on you, your guests, your counters and your furniture. Just another normal part of growing up, and one you need to meet head-on before it becomes an ingrained habit.

The key to jump correction is consistency. You cannot correct your Keeshond for jumping up on you today, then allow it to happen tomorrow by greeting him with hugs and kisses. As you have learned by now, consistency is critical to all puppy lessons.

For starters, try turning your back as soon as the puppy jumps. Jumping up is a means of gaining your attention and, if the pup can't see your face, he may get discouraged and learn that he loses eye contact with his beloved master when he jumps up.

Leash corrections also work, and most puppies respond well to a leash tug if they jump. Grasp the leash close to the puppy's collar and give a quick tug downward, using the command "Off." Do not use the word "Down," since "Down" is used to teach the puppy to lie down, which is a separate action that he will learn during his education in the basic commands. As soon as the puppy has backed off, tell him to sit and immediately praise him for doing so. This will take many repetitions and won't be accomplished quickly, so don't get discouraged or give up; you must be even more persistent than your puppy.

A second method used for jump correction is the spritzer bottle. Fill a spray bottle with water mixed with a bit of lemon juice or vinegar. As soon as puppy jumps, command him "Off" and spritz him with the water mixture. Of course, that means having the spray bottle handy whenever or wherever jumping usually happens.

Yet a third method to discour-

age jumping is grasping the puppy's paws and holding them gently but firmly until he struggles to get away. Wait a brief moment or two, then release his paws and give him a command to sit. He should eventually learn that jumping gets him into an uncomfortable predicament.

Children are major victims of puppy jumping, since puppies view little people as ready targets for jumping up as well as nipping. If your children (or their friends) are unable to dispense jump corrections, you will have to intervene and handle it for them.

Important to prevention is also knowing what you should not do. Never kick your Keeshond (for any reason, not just for jumping) or knock him in the chest with your knee. That maneuver could actually harm your puppy. Vets can tell you stories about puppies who suffered broken bones after being banged about when they jumped up.

Here's a basketful of puppy fun and potential problems. Be prepared for your new arrival. Be informed and ready for whatever your puppy brings with him.

PROPER CARE OF YOUR

KEESHOND

FEEDING THE KEESHOND
Keeshonden are notoriously good eaters. Very few are finicky eaters, and those that are have usually been made so by their owners. Never coax or scold your Kees puppy (or adult for that matter) regarding its eating habits.

FREE-FEEDING
Many owners opt to feed their dogs the free way. That is, they serve dry kibble in a feeder, which is available to the dog all day. Arguably this is the most convenient method of feeding an adult dog, but it may encourage the dog to become fussy about food or defensive over his bowl. Free feeding is only an option for adult dogs, not puppies.

If your adult dog doesn't eat its meal shortly after you have put the food down, take the dish away and do not offer any food until the next regularly scheduled meal time. Only dogs who are not well or who have been terribly spoiled will consistently turn up their nose at food. A sick dog should be taken to the vet. A spoiled dog needs to have its owner retrained.

The best way to make sure your Kees puppy is obtaining the right amount and the correct type of food for its age is to follow the diet sheet provided by the breeder from whom you obtain your puppy. Do your best not to change the puppy's diet and your Kees will be less likely to run into digestive problems and diarrhea.

Generally speaking, a Kees puppy should be fed four times a day until it is approximately three months of age. From three to six months of age, three meals a day (morning, noon and night) are ideal, and from that point on, two meals a day (morning and night) will keep most Kees in fine fettle. When the Keeshond is 12 months of age, feedings can be reduced to once a day; this meal

PUPPY'S FIRST MEAL

Puppies instinctively want to suck milk from their mother's teats; a normal puppy will exhibit this behavior just a few moments following birth. If puppies do not attempt to suckle within the first half-hour or so, they should be encouraged to do so by placing them on the nipples, having selected ones with plenty of milk. This early milk supply is important in providing the essential colostrum, which protects the puppies during the first eight to ten weeks of their lives.

Puppies should be allowed to nurse from their mothers for about the first six weeks, although, starting around the third or fourth week, the breeder will begin to introduce small portions of suitable solid food. Most breeders like to introduce alternate milk and meat meals initially, building up to weaning time. By the time the puppies are seven or a maximum of eight weeks old, they should be fully weaned and fed solely on a proprietary puppy food.

Protein and fat are absolutely essential to the well-being of your dog. A tablespoon of vegetable oil or bacon drippings can be very beneficial, particularly during cold weather.

Read the list of ingredients on the dog food you buy. Animal protein should appear first on the label's list of ingredients. A base of quality kibble to which meat has been added can provide a nutritious meal for your Kees.

Commercial dog foods are produced in three basic types: dried, semi-moist and canned.

The breeder should give you a feeding instruction sheet to provide the basic guidance you need to feed your puppy.

can be given either in the morning or evening. The single meal can be supplemented by a morning or night-time snack of hard dog biscuits made especially for medium- or large-sized dogs.

While the vegetable content of your Kees's diet should not be overlooked, a dog's physiology and anatomy are based upon carnivorous food acquisition.

A row of baby Keeshonds, feeding at mom's milk bank.

Mealtime, naptime or playtime—this baby Kees has had a very busy first day in his new home.

BARF THE WAY TO BETTER HEALTH

That's Biologically Appropriate Raw Food for your dog, as designed and trademarked by Dr. Ian Billinghurst. An alternative to feeding commercially prepared dog foods from a bag or a can that are known to contain numerous additives and preservatives, this diet aims to increase the longevity, overall health and reproductive abilities of dogs. The BARF diet is based on the feeding habits of wild or feral animals and thus includes whole raw animal- and plant-based foods as well as bones. In theory, BARF mimics the natural diets of dogs and contains muscle meat, bone, fat, organ meat and vegetable matter. Many owners are very successful with the diet and others are not. Next time you visit your vet, ask him about BARF.

Dried foods are useful for the cost-conscious, for overall they tend to be less expensive than semi-moist or canned foods. Dried foods also contain the least fat and the most preservatives. In general, canned foods are made up of 60–70% water, while semi-moist ones often contain so much sugar that they are perhaps the least preferred by owners, even though their dogs seem to like them.

It is important to understand that quality commercially prepared foods do contain all the necessary nutrients your Kees needs. It is therefore unnecessary to add vitamin supplements to these diets in other than special circumstances prescribed by your vet.

Over-supplementation and forced growth are now looked upon by some breeders as major contributors to many skeletal abnormalities found in the pure-bred dogs of today. A great deal of controversy exists today regarding orthopedic problems such as hip dysplasia and patellar (knee) luxa-tion, which can afflict all breeds.

Keeping a pack of Keeshonden is a full-time commitment. This group appears to be well trained and wonderfully cared for.

SWITCHING FOODS

There are certain times in a dog's life when it becomes necessary to switch his food; for example, from puppy to adult food and then from adult to senior-dog food. Additionally, you may decide to feed your pup a different type of food from what he received from the breeder, and there may be "emergency" situations in which you can't find your dog's normal brand and have to offer something else temporarily. Any time a change is made, for whatever reason, the switch must be done gradually. You don't want to upset the dog's stomach or end up with a picky eater who refuses to eat something new. A tried-and-true approach is, over the course of about a week, to mix a little of the new food in with the old, increasing the proportion of new to old as the days progress. At the end of the week, you'll be feeding his regular portions of the new food, and he will barely notice the change!

Some claim that these problems are entirely hereditary conditions, but many others feel that they can be exacerbated by over-use of mineral and vitamin supplements for puppies. In giving vitamin supplementation when advised by your vet, never exceed the prescribed amount.

DIETS FOR THE AGING DOG

A good rule of thumb is that once a dog has reached 75% of his expected lifespan, he has reached "senior citizen" or geriatric status, so your Keeshond will be considered a senior at ten years of age.

What does aging have to do with your dog's diet? No, he won't get a discount at the local diner's early-bird special. Yes, he will require some dietary changes to accommodate the changes that come along with increased age. One change is that the older dog's dietary needs become more similar to that of a puppy. Specifically, dogs can metabolize more protein as youngsters and seniors than in the adult-maintenance stage. Discuss with your vet whether you need to switch to a higher protein or senior-formulated food, or if your current adult-dog food contains sufficient nutrition for the senior.

Watching the dog's weight remains essential, even more so in the senior stage. Older dogs are already more vulnerable to illness, and obesity only contributes to his susceptibility to problems. As the older dog becomes less active and thus exercises less, his regular portions may cause him to gain weight. At this point, you may consider decreasing his daily food intake or switching to a reduced-calorie food. As with other changes, you should consult your vet for advice.

DON'T FORGET THE WATER!

For a dog, it's always time for a drink! Regardless of what type of food he eats, there's no doubt that he needs plenty of water. Fresh cold water, in a clean bowl, should be freely available to your dog at all times. There are special circumstances, such as during puppy housebreaking, when you will want to monitor your pup's water intake so that you will be able to predict when he will need to relieve himself, but water must be available to him nonetheless. Water is essential for hydration and proper body function just as it is in humans.

You will get to know how much your dog typically drinks in a day. Of course, in the heat or if exercising vigorously, he will be more thirsty and will drink more. However, if he begins to drink noticeably more water for no apparent reason, this could signal any of various problems, and you are advised to consult your vet.

Water is the best drink for dogs. Some owners are tempted to

NOT HUNGRY?

No dog in his right mind would turn down his dinner, would he? If you notice that your dog has lost interest in his food, there could be any number of causes. Dental problems are a common cause of appetite loss, one that is often overlooked. If your dog has a toothache, a loose tooth or sore gums from infection, chances are it doesn't feel so good to chew. Think about when you've had a toothache! If your dog does not approach the food bowl with his usual enthusiasm, look inside his mouth for signs of a problem. Whatever the cause, you'll want to consult your vet so that your chow hound can get back to his happy, hungry self as soon as possible.

VARIETY IS THE SPICE

Although dog-food manufacturers contend that dogs don't like variety in their diets, studies show quite the opposite to be true. Dogs would much rather vary their meals than eat the same old chow day in and day out. Dry kibble is no more exciting for a dog than the same bowl of bran flakes would be for you. Fortunately, there are dozens of varieties available on the market and your dog will likely show preference for certain flavors over others. A word of warning: don't overdo it or you'll develop a fussy eater who only prefers chopped beef fillet and asparagus tips every night.

with clean fresh water to quench your dog's thirst, and always have it readily available to him.

SPECIAL FEEDING CONSIDERATIONS FOR THE PREGNANT BITCH
To start, a breeding female should be in good bodily condition. To maintain good condition during pregnancy, it is important to consider her individual factors, such as age, metabolism and activity level.

The gestation period is roughly nine weeks, and during the first two trimesters a pregnant bitch's nutritional needs are the same as her regular maintenance diet. However, during the last two or three weeks her requirements increase for all nutrients; this can be achieved by increasing her food intake and making sure she is getting enough protein. As there are foods manufactured for all life stages, there are complete and balanced foods formulated for pregnant bitches. With this type of food, supplementation is not necessary, and too-high levels of certain nutrients can cause problems.

The pregnant female's appetite can fluctuate during pregnancy. At some points she may seem less interested in food but will tend to eat more in the later weeks. This is normal and should not be a concern unless she begins to lose condition. In this case, she must be encouraged to eat, perhaps

give milk from time to time or to moisten dry food with milk, but dogs do not have the enzymes necessary to digest the lactose in milk, which is much different from the milk that nursing puppies receive. Therefore, stick enticing her with moist food or a different flavor to keep up her strength and weight. As whelping approaches, again she may lose her appetite, but this is often a sign that the puppies are on their way within the next day or two.

As with any stage of life, water is essential. In pregnancy it plays the additional role of delivering nutrients to the developing puppies and helping milk production, along with keeping the female in good condition herself.

Milk production is an extra-demanding life stage in terms of nutrition. Her needs can be met with a complete and balanced dog food formulated for reproduction and growth (the same food used during pregnancy is fine), fed in larger amounts than her maintenance diet. This continues for about four weeks after whelping. She may eat as much as four times her normal portion, and she should be allowed as much food as she wants. Proportionate to her increased food intake and to help with milk production, her water needs will increase as well.

As the puppies are weaned, your vet will advise you of dietary changes to aid the dam in slowing milk production and resuming a normal diet.

EXERCISE

Most Kees are very "busy" dogs and remain so even into old age. If your Kees shares his life with

QUENCHING HIS THIRST

Is your dog drinking more than normal and trying to lap up everything in sight? Excessive drinking has many different causes. Obvious causes for a dog's being thirstier than usual are hot weather and vigorous exercise. However, if your dog is drinking more for no apparent reason, you could have cause for concern. Serious conditions like kidney or liver disease, diabetes and various types of hormonal problems can all be indicated by excessive drinking. If you notice your dog's being excessively thirsty, contact your vet at once. Hopefully there will be a simpler explanation, but the earlier a serious problem is detected, the sooner it can be treated with a better rate of cure.

SELECTING THE RIGHT BRUSHES AND COMBS

Will a rubber curry make my dog look slicker? Is a rake smaller than a pin brush? Do I choose nylon or natural bristles? Buying a dog brush can make the hairs on your head stand on end! Here's a quick once-over to educate you on the different types of brushes.

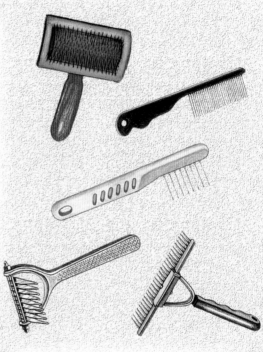

Slicker Brush: Fine metal prongs closely set on a curved base. Used to remove dead coat from the undercoat of medium- to long-coated breeds.

Pin Brush: Metal pins, often covered with rubber tips, set on an oval base. Used to remove shedding hair and is gentler than a slicker brush.

Metal Comb: Steel teeth attached to a steel handle; the closeness and size of the teeth vary greatly. A "flea comb" has tiny teeth set very closely together and is used to find fleas in a dog's coat. Combs with wider teeth are used for detangling longer coats.

Rake: Long-toothed comb with a short handle. Used to remove undercoat from heavily coated breeds with dense undercoats.

Soft-bristle Brush: Nylon or natural bristles set in a plastic or wood base. Used on short coats or long coats (without undercoats).

Rubber Curry: Rubber prongs, with or without a handle. Used for short-coated dogs. Good for use during shampooing.

Combination Brushes: Two-sided brush with a different type of bristle on each side; for example, pin brush on one side and slicker on the other, or bristle brush on one side and pin brush on the other. An economic choice if you need two kinds of brushes.

Grooming Glove: Sometimes called a hound glove, used to give sleek-coated dogs a once-over.

young children or other dogs, he could easily be getting all the exercise he needs to stay fit. A healthy Kees is always ready for a romp or to invent some new game that entails plenty of aerobic activity. This is not to say that your Kees won't benefit by or thoroughly enjoy long hikes, exploring along the beach or wooded trails. Even your "daily constitutional" is something that your Kees will enjoy as much as you will.

Caution must be exercised in hot weather. Remember that the Keeshond is a Nordic dog, accustomed to wintry climes. Plan your walks for the first thing in the morning if at all possible. If you can not arrange to do this, wait until the sun has set and the outdoor temperature has dropped to a comfortable degree. Cold weather, even temperatures hovering around the zero mark, will be no problem at all for a Keeshond. Do not, however, allow your Kees to remain wet if the two of you get caught in the rain. When you return, use a towel or blaster to dry the coat, and then brush your Kees. Doing so will ward off health problems and will avoid mats in the coat.

GROOMING
The Keeshond is a natural breed that requires next to no clipping or trimming. Kees lovers are adamant that the breed not fall into grooming fads of any kind.

Sit your Keeshond puppy on the grooming table. You can keep his feet tidy by scissoring any hair that grows around the pads.

Unless he is going to be entered in a dog show, brushing is all the grooming that your Kees will ever need.

The first piece of equipment you will have to obtain is a grooming table. A grooming table can be built or purchased where you buy pet supplies. Make sure that the table is of a height at which you can work comfortably, either sitting or standing. Adjustable-height grooming tables are available at most pet shops. Anticipate your dog's fully-grown size in making your purchase and select or build a table that will accommodate a fully-grown Kees lying on its side.

You will also need to invest in two brushes, a steel comb, barber's scissors and a pair of nail clippers. The two brushes that you will need are a wire slicker brush (also called a "rake") and a pin brush, sometimes called a "Poodle brush." For the finish work, you will need a commercial coat conditioner and a spray bottle.

START GROOMING LESSONS EARLY

Your job will be considerably eased if your puppy is taught to lie on its side to be groomed. He will be kept in that position for most of the grooming process. Begin this training by picking the puppy up as you would a lamb, with his side against your chest and your arms wrapped around the puppy's body. Lay the puppy down on the table and release your arms, but keep your chest pressed lightly down on the puppy's side. Speak reassuringly to the puppy, stroking his head and rump.

Start with the slicker brush and begin what is called "line-brushing" at the top of the shoulder at the base of the neck. Part the hair in a straight line from the front of the shoulder straight on

SCOOTING HIS BOTTOM

Here's a doggy problem that many owners tend to neglect. If your dog is scooting his rear end around the carpet, he probably is experiencing anal-sac impaction or blockage. The anal sacs are the two grape-sized glands on either side of the dog's vent. The dog cannot empty these glands, which become filled with a foul-smelling material. The dog may attempt to lick the area to relieve the pressure. He may also rub his anus on your walls, furniture or floors.

Don't neglect your dog's rear end during grooming sessions. By squeezing both sides of the anus with a soft cloth, you can express some of the material in the sacs. If the material is pasty and thick, you likely will need the assistance of a veterinarian. Vets know how to express the glands and can show you how to do it correctly without hurting the dog or spraying yourself with poop.

The Keeshond's abundant double coat will require daily grooming, especially during a molt. Keeshonden shed coat twice a year, and the soft, downy undercoat comes out in handfuls.

down to the bottom of the chest. Brush through the hair to the right and left of the part, lightly spraying the area with the coat conditioner as you go. Start at the skin and brush out to the very end of the hair. Do a small section at a time and continue on down the part. When you reach the bottom of the part, return to the top and make another part just to the right of the first line you brushed. Part, brush and spray. You will repeat this process, working toward the rear until you reach the puppy's tail.

Be especially careful to attend to the hard-to-reach areas under the upper legs where they join the body. Mats occur in these areas very rapidly, especially during the time when the Kees is shedding his puppy coat.

Should you encounter a mat that does not brush out easily, use your fingers and the steel comb to separate the hairs as much as possible. Do not cut or pull out the matted hair. Apply baby powder or one of the specially prepared grooming powders directly to the mat and brush completely from the skin out. When you have finished the legs on one side, turn the puppy over and complete the entire process on the other side—part, spray, brush.

While the puppy is sitting, you can do the hair of the chest and neck. Be particularly thorough in the area right behind the ears, as it is highly mat-prone. Use the line-brushing method here as well. Next, stand the puppy up and do the tail. Check the longer hair of the trousers on the rear legs to make sure they are thoroughly brushed, especially around the area of the anus and genitalia. Needless to say, it is important to be extremely careful when brushing in these areas. as they are extremely sensitive and easily injured.

When the line-brushing process is completed, it is time for the finishing touches. Use your barber scissors to trim any long or shaggy hairs around the feet. You may trim off your Kees's whiskers if you wish. This is optional, however. Many Kees owners prefer to leave the whiskers on. Brush the hair around the head, shoulders and back, brushing forward. Do the same with the hair of the tail. Brush the chest hair downward and do the same with the hair on the sides of the puppy.

GROOMING THE ADULT KEESHOND
Not only is the Kees's adult hair of an entirely different texture than that of the puppy, it is much longer and thicker. The pin brush, with its longer bristles set in rubber, is far more effective for line-brushing the adult Kees than the slicker brush that you used on the puppy. The method of brushing the adult coat is the same line-brushing technique that you've used since your Kees was a puppy. The obvious difference is that now you have more dog and more hair.

While one might expect grooming an adult Kees to be a monumental task, this is not necessarily so. The two of you have been practicing the brushing routine for so long that it has undoubtedly become second nature to both of you. Additionally, the adult Kees's hair is actually much easier to manage than the puppy coat. Thoroughly grooming a fully mature Keeshond's coat will take an hour if done no less frequently than weekly. During the twice-yearly shedding period, more time must be invested.

Some misguided owners feel that they are doing their dogs a service by shaving the coats in summer, when exactly the opposite is true. The Kees's coat serves as insulation against both heat and cold, and the Kees's sensitive skin can become sunburned when the dog has been shaved. Never shave a double-coated dog like the Keeshond.

BATHING
In general, dogs need to be bathed only a few times a year, possibly

more often if your dog gets into something messy or if he starts to smell like a dog. Show dogs are usually bathed before every show, which could be as frequent as weekly, although this depends on the owner. Bathing too frequently can have negative effects on the skin and coat, removing natural oils and causing dryness.

If you give your dog his first bath when he is young, he will become accustomed to the process. Wrestling a dog into the tub or chasing a freshly shampooed dog who has escaped from the bath will be no fun! Most dogs don't naturally enjoy their baths, but you at least want him to cooperate with you.

Before bathing the dog, have the items you'll need close at hand. First, decide where you will bathe the dog. You should have a tub or basin with a non-slip surface. Small dogs can even be bathed in a sink. In warm weather, some like to use a portable pool in the yard, although you'll want to make sure your dog doesn't head for the nearest dirt pile following his bath! You will also need a hose or shower spray to wet the coat thoroughly, a shampoo formulated for dogs, absorbent towels and perhaps a blow dryer. Human shampoos are too harsh for dogs' coats and will dry them out.

Before wetting the dog, give him a brush-through to remove

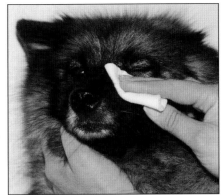

Keep your Keeshond's spectacles unblemished. You can remove tear stains with a soft wipe and a solution available from your local pet shop.

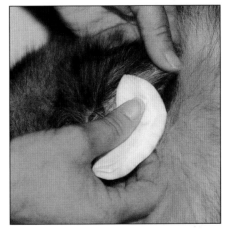

Inspect the dog's ears for any potential parasites, accumulated wax or dirt. A cotton wipe is ideal to wipe the Kees's ear.

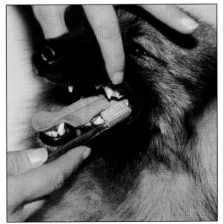

Yes! We brush our Keeshond's teeth, though not as frequently as we brush our own. Attend to your dog's teeth at least once a week to avoid tartar and plaque accumulation.

any dead hair, dirt and mats. Make sure he is at ease in the tub and have the water at a comfortable temperature. Begin bathing by wetting the coat all the way down to the skin. Massage in the shampoo, keeping it away from his face and eyes. Rinse him thoroughly, again avoiding the eyes and ears, as you don't want to get water in the ear canals. A thorough rinsing is important, as shampoo residue is drying and itchy to the dog. After rinsing, wrap him in a towel to absorb the initial moisture. You can finish drying with either a towel or a blow dryer on low heat, held at a safe distance from the dog. You should keep the dog indoors and away from drafts until he is completely dry.

NAIL CLIPPING

Having his nails trimmed is not on many dogs' lists of favorite things to do. With this in mind, you will need to accustom your puppy to the procedure at a young age so that he will sit still (well, as still as he can) for his pedicures. Long nails can cause the dog's feet to spread, which is not good for him; likewise, long nails can hurt if they unintentionally scratch, not good for you!

Some dogs' nails are worn down naturally by regular walking on hard surfaces, so the frequency with which you clip depends on your individual dog. Look at his nails from time to time and clip as needed; a good way to know when it's time for a trim is if you hear your dog clicking as he walks across the floor.

There are several types of nail

THE MONTHLY GRIND

If your dog doesn't like the feeling of nail clippers or if you're not comfortable using them, you may wish to try an electric nail grinder. This tool has a small sandpaper disc on the end that rotates to grind the nails down. Some feel that using a grinder reduces the risk of cutting into the quick; this can be true if the tool is used properly. Usually you will be able to tell where the quick is before you get to it. A benefit of the grinder is that it creates a smooth finish on the nails so that there are no ragged edges.

Because the tool makes noise, your dog should be introduced to it before the actual grinding takes place. Turn it on and let your dog hear the noise; turn it off and let him inspect it with you holding it. Use the grinder gently, holding it firmly and progressing a little at a time until you reach the proper length. Look at the nail as you grind so that you do not go too short. Stop at any indication that you are nearing the quick. It will take a few sessions for both you and the puppy to get used to the grinder. A word of caution with long-coated dogs: do not let his hair get tangled in the grinder!

clippers and even electric nail-grinding tools made for dogs; first we'll discuss using the clipper. To start, have your clipper ready and some doggie treats on hand. You want your pup to view his nail-clipping sessions in a positive light, and what better way to convince him than with food? You may want to enlist the help of an assistant to comfort the pup and offer treats as you concentrate on the clipping itself. The guillotine-type clipper is thought of by many as the easiest type to use; the nail tip is inserted into the opening and blades on the top and bottom snip it off in one clip.

Start by grasping the pup's paw; a little pressure on the foot pad causes the nail to extend, making it easier to clip. Clip off a little at a time. If you can see the "quick," which is a blood vessel that runs through each nail, you will know how much to trim, as you do not want to cut into the quick. On that note, if you do cut the quick, which will cause bleeding, you can stem the flow of blood with a styptic pencil or other clotting agent. If you mistakenly nip the quick, do not panic or fuss, as this will cause the pup to be afraid. Simply reassure the pup, stop the bleeding and move on to the next nail. Don't be discouraged; you will become a professional canine pedicurist with practice.

You may or may not be able to see the quick, so it's best to just clip off a small bit at a time. If you see a dark dot in the center of the nail, this is the quick and your cue to stop clipping. Tell the puppy he's a "good boy" and offer a piece of treat with each nail. You can also use nail-clipping time to examine the footpads, making sure that they are not dry and cracked and that nothing has become embedded in them.

The nail grinder, the second choice, is many owners' first choice. Accustoming the puppy to the sound of the grinder and sensation of the buzz presents fewer challenges than the clipper, and there's no chance of cutting through the quick. Use the grinder on a low setting and always talk soothingly to your dog. He won't mind his salon visit, and he'll have nicely polished nails as well.

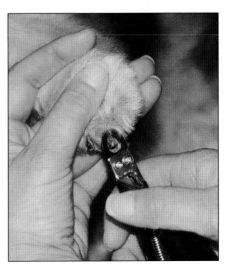

The guillotine-style nail clipper may be the best choice for a Keeshond.

EXTRA SUMMER STRESS

Certain types of dogs encounter more difficulties in the heat and humidity than others; these include young puppies, senior dogs, obese dogs and dogs with short faces. Likewise, if your dog is in poor physical condition or suffering from illness, the heat will take more of a toll on him. Dogs that spend most of their time in the cool climate of air-conditioned homes will be less accustomed to heat and have more problems adjusting.

EAR CLEANING

While keeping your dog's ears clean unfortunately will not cause him to "hear" your commands any better, it will protect him from ear infection and ear-mite infestation. In addition, a dog's ears are vulnerable to waxy build-up and to collecting foreign matter from the outdoors. Look in your dog's ears regularly to ensure that they look pink, clean and otherwise healthy. Even if they look fine, an odor in the ears signals a problem and means it's time to call the vet.

A dog's ears should be cleaned regularly; once a week is suggested, and you can do this along with your regular brushing. Using a cotton ball or pad, and never probing into the ear canal, wipe the ear gently. You can use an ear-cleansing liquid or powder available from your vet or pet-supply store; alternatively, you might prefer to use home-made solutions with ingredients like one part white vinegar and one part hydrogen peroxide. Ask your vet about home remedies before you attempt to concoct something on your own!

Keep your dog's ears free of excess hair by plucking it as needed. If done gently, this will be painless for the dog. Look for wax, brown droppings (a sign of ear mites), redness or any other abnormalities. At the first sign of a problem, contact your vet so that he can prescribe an appropriate medication.

EYE CARE

During grooming sessions, pay extra attention to the condition of your dog's eyes. If the area around the eyes is soiled or if tear staining has occurred, there are various cleaning agents made especially for this purpose. Look at the dog's eyes to make sure no debris has entered; dogs with large eyes and those who spend time outdoors are especially prone to this.

The signs of an eye infection are obvious: mucus, redness, puffiness, scabs or other signs of irritation. If your dog's eyes become infected, the vet will likely prescribe an antibiotic ointment for treatment. If you notice signs of more serious problems, such as opacities in the eye, which usually indicate cataracts, consult the vet at once. Taking time to pay attention to your dog's eyes will alert you in the early stages of any problem so that you can get your dog treatment as soon as possible. You could save your dog's sight!

A Clean Smile

Another essential part of grooming is brushing your dog's teeth and checking his overall oral condition. Studies show that around 80% of dogs experience dental problems by two years of age, and the percentage is higher in older dogs. Therefore it is highly likely that your dog will have trouble with his teeth and gums unless you are proactive with home dental care.

The most common dental problem in dogs is plaque build-up. If not treated, this causes gum disease, infection and resultant tooth loss. Bacteria from these infections spread throughout the body, affecting the vital organs. Do you need much more convincing to start brushing your dog's teeth? If so, take a good whiff of your dog's breath, and read on.

Fortunately, home dental care is rather easy and convenient for pet owners. Specially formulated canine toothpaste is easy to find. You should use dog toothpaste, not a product for humans. Some doggie pastes are even available in flavors appealing to dogs. If he likes the flavor, he will tolerate the process better, making things much easier for you! Doggie toothbrushes come in different sizes and are designed to fit the contour of a canine mouth. Rubber fingertip brushes fit right on one of your fingers and have rubber nodes to

PRESERVING THOSE PEARLY WHITES

What do you treasure more than the smile of your beloved canine pal? Brushing your dog's teeth is just as important as brushing your own. Neglecting your dog's teeth can lead to tooth loss, periodontal disease and inflamed gums, not to mention bad breath. Can you find the time to brush your dog's teeth every day? If not, you should do so once a week at the very least, though every day is truly the ideal. Your vet should give your dog a thorough dental examination during his annual check-ups.

THE EARS KNOW

Examining your puppy's ears helps ensure good internal health. The ears are the eyes to the dog's innards! Begin handling your puppy's ears when he's still young so that he doesn't protest every time you lift a flap or touch his ears. Yeast and bacteria are two of the culprits that you can detect by examining the ear. You will notice a strong, often foul, odor, debris, redness or some kind of discharge. All of these point to health problems that can worsen over time. Additionally, you are on the lookout for wax accumulation, ear mites and other tiny bothersome parasites and their even tinier droppings. Kees have well-furred ears, so you may have to pluck hair with tweezers in order to have a better view into your dog's ears, but this is painless if done carefully.

clean the teeth and massage the gums. This may be easier to handle, as it is akin to rubbing your dog's teeth with your finger.

As with other grooming tasks, accustom your pup to his dental care early on. Start gently, for a few minutes at a time, so that he gets used to the feel of the brush and to your handling his mouth. Offer praise and petting so that he looks at tooth-care time as a time when he gets extra love and attention. The routine should become second nature; at the very least, he should be willing to tolerate it.

Aside from brushing, offer dental toys to your dog and feed crunchy biscuits, which help to minimize plaque. Rope toys have the added benefit of acting like floss as the dog chews. At your adult dog's yearly check-ups, the vet will likely perform a thorough tooth scraping as well as a complete check for any problems. Proper care of your dog's teeth will ensure that you will enjoy your dog's smile for many years to come. The next time your dog goes to give you a hello kiss, you'll be glad you spent the time caring for his teeth.

THE OTHER END

Dogs sometime have troubles with their anal glands, which are sacs located beside the anal vent. These should empty when a dog has normal bowel movements but, if not, they can become full or impacted, causing discomfort. Owners often are alarmed to see their dogs scooting across the floor, dragging their behinds behind! This is a dog's attempt to empty the glands himself.

Some brave owners attempt to evacuate their dogs' anal glands themselves during grooming, but no one will tell you that this is a pleasant task! Thus, many owners prefer to make the trip to the vet to have the vet take care of the problem; owners whose dogs visit a groomer can have this done by the groomer if he offers this as part of his services. Regardless, don't neglect the dog's other end in your home-care routine. Look for scooting, licking or other signs of discomfort "back there" to ascertain if the anal glands need to be emptied.

BASIC TRAINING PRINCIPLES: PUPPY VS. ADULT

There's a big difference between training an adult dog and training a young puppy. With a young puppy, everything is new! At eight to ten weeks of age, he will be experiencing many things, and he has nothing to which to compare these experiences. Up to this point he has been with his dam and littermates, not one-on-one with people, except in his interactions with his breeder and visitors to the litter.

When you first bring the puppy home, he is eager to please you. This means that he accepts doing things your way! During the next couple of months, he will absorb the basis of everything he needs to know for the rest of his

life. This early age is even referred to as the "sponge" stage. After that, for the next 18 months, it's up to you to reinforce good manners by building on the foundation that you've established. Once your puppy is reliable in basic commands and behavior,

You could not ask for a more attentive and trainable student than the Keeshond. The Keeshond is likely the most trainable of all the spitz breeds.

OUR CANINE KIDS

"Everything I learned about parenting, I learned from my dog." How often adults recognize that their parenting skills are mere extensions of the education they acquired while caring for their dogs. Many owners refer to their dogs as their "kids" and treat their canine companions like real members of the family. Surveys indicate that a majority of dog owners talk to their dogs regularly, celebrate their dogs' birthdays and purchase Christmas gifts for their dogs. Another survey shows that dog owners take their dogs to the veterinarian more frequently than they visit their own physicians.

and has reached the appropriate age, you may gradually introduce him to some of the interesting sports, games and activities available to pet owners and their dogs.

Raising your puppy is a

family affair. Each member of the family must know what rules to set forth for the puppy and how to use the same one-word commands to mean exactly the same thing every time. Even if yours is a large family, one person will soon be considered by the pup to be the leader, the Alpha person in his pack, the "boss" who must be obeyed. Often that highly regarded person turns out to be the one who feeds the puppy. Food ranks very high on the puppy's list of important things! That's why your puppy is rewarded with small treats along with verbal praise when he responds to you correctly. As the puppy learns to do what you want him to do, the food rewards are gradually eliminated and only the praise remains. If you keep up with the food treats, you could have two problems on your hands—an obese dog and a beggar.

Training begins the minute your puppy steps through the doorway of your home, so don't make the mistake of putting the puppy on the floor and telling him by your actions, "Go for it! Run wild!" Even if this is your first puppy, you must act as if you know what you're doing: be the boss. An uncertain pup may be terrified to move, while a bold one will be ready to take you at your word and start plotting to destroy the house! Before you collected

BASIC PRINCIPLES OF DOG TRAINING

1. Start training early. A young puppy is ready, willing and able.
2. Timing is your all-important tool. Praise at the exact time that the dog responds correctly. Pay close attention.
3. Patience is almost as important as timing!
4. Repeat! The same word has to mean the same thing every time. Puppies often play the "Oh, I forgot!" game.
5. In the beginning, praise all correct behavior verbally, along with treats and petting.

your puppy, you decided where his own special place would be, and that's where to put him when you first arrive home. Give him a house tour after he has investigated his area and had a nap and a bathroom "pit stop."

It's worth mentioning here that if you've adopted an adult dog that is completely trained to your liking, lucky you! You're off the hook! However, if that dog spent his life up to this point in a kennel, or even in a good home but without any real training, be prepared to tackle the job ahead. A dog three years of age or older with no previous training cannot be blamed for not knowing what he was never taught. While the dog is trying to understand and learn your rules, at the same time he has to unlearn many of his previously self-taught habits and general view of the world.

Working with a professional trainer will speed up your progress with an adopted adult dog. You'll need patience, too. Some new rules may be close to impossible for the dog to accept. After all, he's been successful so far by doing everything his way! (Patience again.) He may agree with your instruction for a few days and then slip back into his old ways, so you must be just as consistent and understanding in your teaching as you would be with a puppy. (More patience needed yet again!) Your dog has to

THE RIGHT START

The best advice for a potential dog owner is to start with the very best puppy that money can buy. Don't shop around for a bargain in the newspaper. You're buying a companion, not a used Buick or a second-hand Maytag. The purchase price of the dog represents a very significant part of the investment, but this is indeed a very small sum compared to the expenses of maintaining the dog in good health. If you purchase a well-bred, healthy and sound puppy, you will be starting right. An unhealthy puppy can cost you thousands of dollars in unnecessary veterinary expenses and, possibly, a fortune in heartbreak as well.

learn to pay attention to your voice, your family, the daily routine, new smells, new sounds and, in some cases, even a new climate.

One of the most important things to find out about a newly

adopted adult dog is his reaction to children (yours and others), strangers and your friends, and how he acts upon meeting other dogs. If he was not socialized with dogs as a puppy, this could be a major problem. This does not mean that he's a "bad" dog, a vicious dog or an aggressive dog;

rather, it means that he has no idea how to read another dog's body language. There's no way for him to tell if the other dog is a friend or foe. Survival instinct takes over, telling him to attack first and ask questions later. This definitely calls for professional help and, even then, may not be a behavior that can be corrected 100% reliably (or even at all). If you have a puppy, this is why it is so very important to introduce your young puppy properly to other puppies and "dog-friendly" adult dogs.

DAILY SCHEDULE

How many relief trips does your puppy need per day? A puppy up to the age of 14 weeks will need to go outside about 8 to 12 times per day! You will have to take the pup out any time he starts sniffing around the floor or turning in small circles, as well as after naps, meals, games and lessons or whenever he's released from his crate. Once the puppy is 14 to 22 weeks of age, he will only require 6 to 8 relief trips. At the ages of 22 to 32 weeks, the puppy will require about 5 to 7 trips. Adult dogs typically require 4 relief trips per day, in the morning, afternoon, evening and late at night.

HOUSE-TRAINING

Dogs are tactility-oriented when it comes to house-training. In other words, they respond to the surface on which they are given approval to eliminate. The choice is yours (the dog's version is in parentheses): The lawn (including the neighbors' lawns)? A bare patch of earth under a tree (where people like to sit and relax in the summertime)? Concrete steps or patio (all sidewalks, garage and basement floors)? The curbside (watch out for cars)? A small area of crushed stone in a corner of the yard (mine!)? The latter is the best choice if you can manage it, because it will remain strictly for the dog's use and is easy to keep clean.

You can start out with paper-training indoors and switch over to an outdoor surface as the

puppy matures and gains control over his need to eliminate. For the nay-sayers, don't worry—this won't mean that the dog will soil on every piece of newspaper lying around the house. You are training him to go outside, remember? Starting out by paper-training often is the only choice for a city dog.

WHEN YOUR PUPPY'S "GOT TO GO"
Your puppy's need to relieve himself is seemingly non-stop, but signs of improvement will be seen each week. From 8 to 10 weeks old, the puppy will have to be taken outside every time he wakes up, about 10-15 minutes after every meal and after every period of play—all day long, from first thing in the morning until his bedtime! That's a total of ten or more trips per day to teach the puppy where it's okay to relieve himself. With that schedule in mind, you can see that house-training a young puppy is not a part-time job. It requires someone to be home all day.

If that seems overwhelming or impossible, do a little planning. For example, plan to pick up your puppy at the start of a vacation period. If you can't get home in the middle of the day, plan to hire a dog-sitter or ask a neighbor to come over to take the pup outside, feed him his lunch and then take him out again about ten or so minutes after he's eaten. Also

TIDY BOY
Clean by nature, dogs do not like to soil their dens, which in effect are their crates or sleeping quarters. Unless not feeling well, dogs will not defecate or urinate in their crates. Crate training capitalizes on the dog's natural desire to keep his den clean. Be conscientious about giving the puppy as many opportunities to relieve himself outdoors as possible. Reward the puppy for correct behavior. Praise him and pat his head whenever he "goes" in the correct location. Even the tidiest of puppies can have potty accidents, so be patient and dedicate more energy to helping your puppy achieve a clean lifestyle.

make arrangements with that or another person to be your "emergency" contact if you have to stay late on the job. Remind yourself—repeatedly—that this hectic schedule improves as the puppy gets older.

HOME WITHIN A HOME

Your puppy needs to be confined to one secure, puppy-proof area when no one is able to watch his every move. Generally, the kitchen is the place of choice because the floor is washable. Likewise, it's a busy family area that will accustom the pup to a variety of noises, everything from pots and pans to the telephone, blender and dishwasher. He will also be enchanted by the smell of your cooking (and will never be critical when you burn something). An exercise pen (also called an "ex-pen," a puppy version of a playpen) within the room of choice is an excellent means of confinement for a young pup. He can see out and has a certain amount of space in which

No matter how portable your cuddly Kees is, do not carry him to his toilet area. Use a leash and let him walk.

LEASH TRAINING

House-training and leash training go hand in hand, literally. When taking your puppy outside to do his business, lead him there on his leash. Unless an emergency potty run is called for, do not whisk the puppy in your arms and take him outside. If you have a fenced yard, you have the advantage of letting the puppy loose to go out, but it's better to put the dog on the leash and take him to his designated place in the yard until he is reliably house-trained. Taking the puppy for a walk is the best way to house-train a dog. The dog will associate the walk with his time to relieve himself, and the exercise of walking stimulates the dog's bowels and bladder. Dogs that are not trained to relieve themselves on a walk may hold it until they get back home, which of course defeats half the purpose of the walk.

to run about, but he is safe from dangerous things like electrical cords, heating units, trash baskets or open kitchen-supply cabinets. Place the pen where the puppy will not get a blast of heat or air conditioning.

In the pen, you can put a few toys, his bed (which can be his crate if the dimensions of pen and crate are compatible) and a few layers of newspaper in one small corner, just in case. A water bowl can be hung at a convenient height on the side of the ex-pen so it won't become a splashing pool for an innovative puppy. His food dish can go on the floor, next to the water bowl.

Crates are something that pet owners are at last getting used to for their dogs. Wild or domestic canines have always preferred to sleep in den-like safe spots, and that is exactly what the crate provides. How often have you seen adult dogs that choose to sleep under a table or chair even though they have full run of the house? It's the den connection.

The crate can be solid (fiberglass) with ventilation on the upper sides and a wire-grate door that locks securely, or it can be of open wire construction with a solid floor. Your puppy will go along with whichever one you prefer. The open wire crate, however, should be covered at night to give the snug feeling of a den. A blanket or towel over the top will be fine.

The crate should be big enough for the adult dog to stand up and turn around in, even though he may spend much of his time curled up in the back part of it. There are movable barriers that fit inside dog crates to provide the right amount of space for small puppies that grow into large dogs. Never afford a young puppy too much space thinking that you're being kind and generous. He'll just sleep at one end of the crate and soil in the other end! While you should purchase only one crate, one that will accommodate your pup when grown, you will need to make use of the partitions so that the pup has a comfortable area without enough extra space to use as a toilet. A dog does not like to soil where he sleeps, so

SOMEBODY TO BLAME

House-training a puppy can be frustrating for the puppy and the owner alike. The puppy does not instinctively understand the difference between defecating on the pavement outside and piddling on the ceramic tile in the kitchen. He is confused and frightened by his human's exuberant reactions to his natural urges. The owner, arguably the more intelligent of the duo, is also frustrated that he cannot convince his puppy to obey his commands and instructions.

In frustration, the owner may struggle with the temptation to discipline the puppy, scold him or even strike the puppy on the rear end. Shouting and smacking the puppy may make you feel better, but it will defeat your purpose in gaining your puppy's trust and respect. Don't blame your nine-week-old puppy. Blame yourself for not being 100% consistent in the puppy's lessons and routine. The lesson here is simple: try harder and your puppy will succeed in proportion to your efforts.

you are teaching him to "hold it" until it's time for a trip outside. You may want an extra crate to keep in the car for safe traveling.

In your "happy" voice, use the word "Crate" every time you put the pup into his den. If he's new to a crate, toss in a small biscuit for him to chase the first few times. At night, after he's been outside, he should sleep in his crate. The crate may be kept in his designated area at night or, if you want to be sure to hear those wake-up yips in the morning, put the crate in a corner of your bedroom. However, don't make any response whatsoever to whining or crying. If he's completely ignored, he'll settle down and get to sleep.

Good bedding for a young puppy is an old folded bath towel or an old blanket, something that is easily washable and disposable if necessary ("accidents" will happen!). Never put newspaper into the puppy's crate. Those old ideas of adding a clock to replace his mother's heartbeat, or a hot-water bottle to replace her warmth, are just that—old ideas. The clock could drive the puppy nuts, and the hot-water bottle could end up as a very soggy waterbed! An extremely good breeder would have introduced your puppy to the crate by letting two pups sleep together for a couple of nights, followed by several nights alone. How thank-

POTTY COMMAND

Most dogs love to please their masters and there are no bounds to what dogs will do to make their owners happy. The potty command is a good example of this theory. If toileting on command makes the master happy, then more power to him. Puppies will obligingly piddle if it really makes their keepers smile. Some owners can be creative about which word they will use to command their dogs to relieve themselves. Some popular choices are "Potty," "Tinkle," "Piddle," "Let's go," "Hurry up" and "Toilet." Give the command every time your puppy goes into position and the puppy will begin to associate his business with the command.

ful you will be if you found that breeder!

Safe toys in the pup's crate or area will keep him occupied, but monitor their condition closely. Discard any toys that show signs of being chewed to bits. Squeaky parts, bits of stuffing or plastic or any other small pieces can cause intestinal blockage or possibly choking if swallowed.

PROGRESSING WITH POTTY-TRAINING

After you've taken your puppy out and he has relieved himself in the area you've selected, he can have some free time with the

"Down" is the command used to have the dog assume this posture. "Off" means stop doing what you're doing.

family as long as there is someone responsible for watching him. That doesn't mean just someone in the same room who is watching TV or busy on the computer, but one person who is doing nothing other than keeping an eye on the pup, playing with him on the floor and helping him understand his position in the pack.

This first taste of freedom will let you begin to set the house rules. If you don't want the dog on the furniture, now is the time to prevent his first attempts to jump up onto the couch. The word to use in this case is "Off," not "Down." "Down" is the word you will use to teach the down position, which is something entirely different.

Most corrections at this stage come in the form of simply distracting the puppy. Instead of telling him "No" for "Don't chew the carpet," distract the chomping puppy with a toy and he'll forget about the carpet.

As you are playing with the pup, do not forget to watch him closely and pay attention to his body language. Whenever you see him begin to circle or sniff, take the puppy outside to relieve himself. If you are paper-training, put him back into his confined area on the newspapers. In either case, praise him as he eliminates while he actually is in the act of relieving himself. Three seconds after he has finished is too late! You'll be praising him for running toward you, or picking up a toy or whatever he may be doing at that moment, and that's not what you want to be praising him for. Timing is a vital tool in all dog training. Use it!

Remove soiled newspapers immediately and replace them with clean ones. You may want to take a small piece of soiled paper and place it in the middle of the new clean papers, as the scent will attract him to that spot when it's time to go again. That scent attraction is why it's so important to clean up any messes made in the house by using a product specially made to eliminate the odor of dog urine and droppings. Regular household cleansers won't do the trick. Pet shops sell the best pet deodorizers. Invest in the largest container you can find.

Scent attraction eventually will lead your pup to his chosen spot outdoors; this is the basis of outdoor training. When you take your puppy outside to relieve himself, use a one-word command such as "Outside" or "Go-potty" (that's one word to the puppy!) as you pick him up and attach his leash. Then put him down in his area. If he is too big for you to carry, snap the leash on quickly and lead him to his spot. Now comes the hard part—hard for you, that is. Just stand there until he urinates and defecates. Move

CREATURES OF HABIT
Canine behaviorists and trainers aptly describe dogs as "creatures of habit," meaning that dogs respond to structure in their daily lives and welcome a routine. Do not interpret this to mean that dogs enjoy endless repetition in their training sessions. Dogs get bored just as humans do. Keep training sessions interesting and exciting. Vary the commands and the locations in which you practice. Give short breaks for play in between lessons. A bored student will never be the best performer in the class.

him a few feet in one direction or another if he's just sitting there looking at you, but remember that this is neither playtime nor time for a walk. This is strictly a business trip! Then, as he circles and squats (remember your timing!), give him a quiet "Good dog" as praise. If you start to jump for joy, ecstatic over his performance, he'll do one of two things: either he will stop mid-stream, as it were, or he'll do it again for you—in the house—and expect you to be just as delighted!

Give him five minutes or so and, if he doesn't go in that time, take him back indoors to his confined area and try again in another ten minutes, or immediately if you see him sniffing and circling. By careful observation, you'll soon work out a successful schedule.

Accidents, by the way, are just that—accidents. Clean them up quickly and thoroughly, without comment, after the puppy has been taken outside to finish his business and then put back into his area or crate. If you witness an accident in progress, say "No!" in a stern voice and get the pup outdoors immediately. No punishment is needed. You and your puppy are just learning each other's language, and sometimes it's easy to miss a puppy's message. Chalk it up to experience and watch more closely from now on.

KEEPING THE PACK ORDERLY

Discipline is a form of training that brings order to life. For example, military discipline is what allows the soldiers in an army to work as one. Discipline is a form of teaching and, in dogs, is the basis of how the successful pack operates. Each member knows his place in the pack and all respect

RIGHT CLICK ON YOUR DOG

With three clicks, the dolphin jumps through the hoop. Wouldn't it be nice to have a dog who could obey wordless commands that easily? Clicker training actually was developed by dolphin trainers and today is used on dogs with great success. You can buy a clicker at a pet shop or pet-supply outlet, and then you'll be off and clicking.

You can click your dog into learning new commands, shaping or conditioning his behavior and solving bad habits. The clicker, used in conjunction with a treat, is an extension of positive reinforcement. The dog begins to recognize your happy clicking, and you will never have to use physical force again. The dog is conditioned to follow your hand with the clicker, just as he would follow your hand with a treat. To discourage the dog from inappropriate behavior (like jumping up or barking), you can use the clicker to set a timeframe and then click and reward the dog once he's waited the allotted time without jumping up or barking.

Each member of the litter (or pack) looks up to the dam for guidance, protection and food. Your new pack member will rely upon you for all of these needs and more.

the leader, or Alpha dog. It is essential for your puppy that you establish this type of relationship, with you as the Alpha, or leader. It is a form of social coexistence that all canines recognize and accept. Discipline, therefore, is never to be confused with punishment. When you teach your puppy how you want him to behave, and he behaves properly and you praise him for it, you are disciplining him with a form of positive reinforcement.

For a dog, rewards come in the form of praise, a smile, a cheerful tone of voice, a few friendly pats or a rub of the ears. Rewards are also small food treats. Obviously, that does not mean bits of regular dog food. Rather, treats are very small bits of special things like cheese or pieces of soft dog treats. The idea is to reward the dog with something very small that he can taste and swallow, providing instant positive reinforcement. If he has to take time to chew the treat, by the time he is finished he will have forgotten what he did to earn it!

Your puppy should never be physically punished. The displeasure shown on your face and in your voice is sufficient to signal to the pup that he has done something wrong. He wants to please everyone higher up on the social ladder, especially his leader, so a scowl and harsh voice will take care of the error. Growling out the word "Shame!" when the pup is caught in the act of doing something wrong is better than the repetitive "No." Some dogs hear "No" so often that they begin to think it's their name! By the way, do not use the dog's name when you're correcting him. His name is reserved to get his attention for something pleasant about to take place.

There are punishments that have nothing to do with you. For example, your dog may think that chasing cats is one reason for his existence. You can try to stop it as much as you like without success because it's such fun for the dog. But one good hissing, spitting, swipe of a cat's claws across the dog's nose will put an end to the

WHO'S TRAINING WHOM?

Dog training is a black-and-white exercise. The correct response to a command must be absolute, and the trainer must insist on completely accurate responses from the dog. A trainer cannot command his dog to sit and settle for the dog's melting into the down position. Often owners are so pleased that their dogs "did something" in response to a command that they just shrug and say, "OK, down" even though they wanted the dog to sit. You want your dog to respond to the command without hesitation: he must respond at that moment and correctly every time.

game forever. Only intervene when your dog's eyeball is seriously at risk. Cat scratches can cause permanent damage to an innocent but annoying puppy.

PUPPY KINDERGARTEN

COLLAR AND LEASH

Before you begin your puppy's education, he must be used to his collar and leash. Choose a collar for your puppy that is secure, but not heavy or bulky. He won't enjoy training if he's uncomfortable. A flat buckle collar is fine for everyday wear and for initial puppy training. For older dogs, there are several types of training collars such as the martingale, which is a double loop that tightens slightly around the neck, or the head collar, which is similar to a horse's halter. Do not use a chain choke collar unless you have been specifically shown how to put it on and how to use it. Coated breeds like the Keeshond are not suitable for chain chokes.

A lightweight 6-foot woven cotton or nylon training leash is preferred by most trainers because it is easy to fold up in your hand and comfortable to hold because there is a certain amount of give to it. There are lessons where the dog will start off six feet away from you at the end of the leash. The leash used to take the puppy outside to relieve himself is shorter because you don't want

A treat can help maintain your Kees's attention. In the dog world, bribery is an art form.

him to roam away from his area. The shorter leash will also be the one to use when you walk the puppy, for the same reason.

If you've been fortunate enough to enroll in a Puppy Kindergarten training class, suggestions will be made as to the best collar and leash for your young puppy. I say "fortunate" because your puppy will be in a class with puppies in his age range (up to five months old) of all breeds and sizes. It's the perfect way for him to learn the right way (and the wrong way) to interact with other dogs as well as their people. You cannot teach your puppy how to interpret another dog's sign language. For a first-time puppy owner, these socialization classes are invaluable. For experienced dog owners, they are a real boon to further training.

"Sit" is a very good place to start, as it's a natural comfortable position for a dog.

ATTENTION

You've been using the dog's name since the minute you collected him from the breeder, so you should be able to get his attention by saying his name—with a big smile and in an excited tone of voice. His response will be the puppy equivalent of "Here I am! What are we going to do?" Your immediate response (if you haven't guessed by now) is "Good dog." Rewarding him at the moment he pays attention to you teaches him the proper way to respond when he hears his name.

EXERCISES FOR A BASIC CANINE EDUCATION

THE SIT EXERCISE

There are several ways to teach the puppy to sit. The first one is to catch him whenever he is about to sit and, as his backside nears the floor, say "Sit, good dog!" That's positive reinforcement and, if your timing is sharp, he will learn that what he's doing at that second is connected to your saying "Sit" and that you think he's clever for doing it!

Another method is to start with the puppy on his leash in front of you. Show him a treat in the palm of your right hand. Bring your hand up under his nose and, almost in slow motion, move your hand up and back so his nose goes up in the air and his head tilts back as he follows the treat in your hand. At that point, he will have to either sit or fall over, so as his back legs buckle under, say "Sit, good dog," and then give him the treat and lots of praise. You may have to begin with your hand lightly running up his chest, actually lifting his chin up until he sits. Some (usually older) dogs require gentle pressure on their hindquarters with the left hand, in which case the dog should be on your left side. Puppies gener-

SMILE WHEN YOU ORDER ME AROUND!

While trainers recommend practicing with your dog every day, it's perfectly acceptable to take a "mental health day" off. It's better not to train the dog on days when you're in a sour mood. Your bad attitude or lack of interest will be sensed by your dog, and he will respond accordingly. Studies show that dogs are well tuned in to their humans' emotions. Be conscious of how you use your voice when talking to your dog. Raising your voice or shouting will only erode your dog's trust in you as his trainer and master.

ally do not appreciate this physical dominance.

After a few times, you should be able to show the dog a treat in the open palm of your hand, raise your hand waist-high as you say "Sit" and have him sit. Once again, you have taught him two things at the same time. The verbal command and the motion of the hand are both signals for the sit. Your puppy is watching you almost more than he is listening to you, so what you do is just as important as what you say.

Don't save any of these drills only for training sessions. Use them as much as possible at odd times during a normal day. The dog should always sit before being given his food dish. He should sit to let you go through a doorway first, when the doorbell rings or when you stop to speak to someone on the street.

THE DOWN EXERCISE

Before beginning to teach the down command, you must

The sit command is necessary for every canine citizen. Once the exercise has been mastered, the dog will respond to the command instantly (without a reward).

consider how the dog feels about this exercise. To him, "down" is a submissive position. Being flat on the floor with you standing over him is not his idea of fun. It's up to you to let him know that, while it may not be fun, the reward of your approval is worth his effort.

Start with the puppy on your left side in a sit position. Hold the leash right above his collar in your left hand. Have an extra-special treat, such as a small piece of cooked chicken or hot dog, in your right hand. Place it at the end of the pup's nose and steadily move your hand down and forward along the ground. Hold the leash to prevent a sudden lunge for the food. As the puppy goes into the down position, say

Use a food treat to encourage the dog to assume the down position.

The hand signal effectively relays to the Keeshond that he should stay ("stop" and "do nothing").

"Down" very gently.

The difficulty with this exercise is twofold: it's both the submissive aspect and the fact that most people say the word "Down" as if they were a drill sergeant in charge of recruits! So issue the command sweetly, give him the treat and have the pup maintain the down position for several seconds. If he tries to get up immediately, place your hands on his shoulders and press down gently, giving him a very quiet "Good dog." As you progress with this lesson, increase the "down time" until he will hold it until you say "Okay" (his cue for release). Practice this one in the house at various times throughout the day.

By increasing the length of time during which the dog must maintain the down position, you'll find many uses for it. For example, he can lie at your feet in the vet's office or anywhere that both of you have to wait, when you are on the phone, while the family is eating and so forth. If you progress to training for competitive obedience, he'll already be all set for the exercise called the "long down."

THE STAY EXERCISE

Let's begin with the sit/stay command, even though you can teach your Kees to stay in any position. To teach the sit/stay, have the dog sit on your left side. Hold the leash at waist level in your left hand and let the dog know that you have a treat in your closed right hand. Step forward on your right foot as you say "Stay." Immediately turn and stand directly in front of the dog, keeping your right hand up high so he'll keep his eye on the treat hand and maintain the sit position for a count of five. Return to

KEEP IT SIMPLE—AND FUN

Practicing obedience is not a military drill. Keep your lessons simple, interesting and user-friendly. Fun breaks help you both. Spend two minutes or ten teaching your puppy, but only practice as long as your dog enjoys what he's doing and is focused on pleasing you. If he's bored or distracted, stop the training session after any correct response (always end on a high note!). After a few minutes of playtime, you can go back to "hitting the books."

OKAY!

This is the signal that tells your dog that he can quit whatever he was doing. Use "Okay" to end a session on a correct response to a command. (Never end on an incorrect response.) Lots of praise follows. People use "Okay" a lot and it has other uses for dogs, too. Your dog is barking. You say, "Okay! Come!" "Okay" signals him to stop the barking activity and "Come" allows him to come to you for a "Good dog."

your original position and offer the reward.

Increase the length of the sit/stay each time until the dog can hold it for at least 30 seconds without moving. After about a week of success, move out on your right foot and take two steps before turning to face the dog. Give the "Stay" hand signal (left palm back toward the dog's head) as you leave. He gets the treat when you return and he holds the sit/stay. Increase the distance that you walk away from him before turning until you reach the length of your training leash. But don't rush it! Go back to the beginning if he moves before he should. No matter what the lesson, never be upset by having to back up for a few days. The repetition and practice are what will make your dog reliable in these commands. It won't do any good to move on to something more difficult if the command is not mastered at the easier levels. Above all, even if you do get frustrated, never let your puppy know! Always keep a positive, upbeat attitude during training, which will transmit to your dog for positive results!

The down/stay is taught in the same way once the dog is completely reliable and steady with the down command. Again, don't rush it. With the dog in the down position on your left side, step out on your right foot as you say "Stay." Return by walking around in back of the dog and into your original position. While you are training, it's okay to murmur something like "Hold on" to encourage him to stay put. When the dog will stay without

The attentive Kees student will watch his owner for the next command.

moving when you are at a distance of 3 or 4 feet, begin to increase the length of time before you return. Be sure he holds the down on your return until you say "Okay." At that point, he gets his treat–just so he'll remember for next time that it's not over until it's over.

THE COME EXERCISE

No command is more important to the safety of your dog than "Come." It is what you should say every single time you see the puppy running toward you: "Binky, come! Good dog." During playtime, run a few feet away from the puppy, turn and tell him to "Come" as he is already running to you. You can go so far as to teach your puppy two things at once if you squat down and hold out your arms. As the pup gets close to you and you're saying "Good dog," bring your right arm in about waist high. Now he's also learning the hand signal, an excellent device should

Positive reinforcement and cheerful praise insure that your Kees will come to you every time.

> **I WILL FOLLOW YOU**
> Obedience isn't just a classroom activity. In your home, you have many great opportunities to teach your dog polite manners. Allowing your pet on the bed or furniture elevates him to your level, which is not a good idea (the word is "Off!"). Use the "umbilical cord" method, keeping your dog on lead so he has to go with you wherever you go. You sit, he sits. You walk, he heels. You stop, he sit-stays. Everywhere you go, he's with you, but you go first!

you be on the phone when you need to get him to come to you! You'll also both be one step ahead when you enter obedience classes.

Puppies, like children, have notoriously short attention spans, so don't overdo it with any of the training. Keep each lesson short. Break it up with a quick run around the yard or a ball toss, repeat the lesson and quit as soon as the pup gets it right. That way, you will always end with a "Good dog."

When the puppy responds to your well-timed "Come," try it with the puppy on the training leash. This time, catch him off guard, while he's sniffing a leaf or watching a bird: "Binky, come!" You may have to pause for a split second after his name to be sure you have his attention. If the puppy shows any sign of confusion, give the leash a mild jerk and take a couple of steps backward. Do not repeat the command. In this case, as he reaches you you should say "Good come!"

That's the number-one rule of training. Each command word is given just once. Anything more is nagging. You'll also notice that all commands are one word only. Even when they are actually two words, you say them as one.

Never call the dog to come to you—with or without his name—if you are angry or intend to correct him for some misbehavior. When correcting the pup, you go to him. Your dog must always connect "come" with something pleasant and with your approval; then you can rely on his response. Life isn't perfect and neither are puppies. A time will come, often around 10 months of age, when he'll become "selectively deaf" or choose to "forget" his name. He may respond by wagging his tail (and even seeming to smile at you) with a look that says "Make me!" Laugh, throw his favorite toy and skip the lesson you had planned. Pups will be pups!

THE HEEL EXERCISE

The second most important command to teach, after the come, is the heel. When you are walking your growing puppy, you need to be in control. Besides, it looks terrible to be pulled and yanked

Keep the Kees on your left side when practicing the heel exercise.

down the street, and it's not much fun either! Your eight-to ten-week old puppy will probably follow you everywhere, but that's his natural instinct, not your control over the situation. However, any time he does follow you, you can say "Heel" and be ahead of the game, as he will learn to associate this command with the action of following you before you even begin teaching him to heel.

There is a very precise, almost military, procedure for teaching your dog to heel. As with other obedience training, begin with the dog on your left side. He will be in a very nice sit and you will have the training leash across your chest. Hold the loop and folded leash in your right hand. Pick up the slack leash above the dog in

A well-trained Kees is a pleasure to walk. Heel training makes your dog's everyday walk an activity that you both will look forward to.

your left hand and hold it loosely at your side. Step out on your left foot as you say "Heel." If the puppy does not move, give a gentle tug or pat your left leg to get him started. If he surges ahead of you, stop and pull him back gently until he is at your side. Tell him to sit and begin again.

Walk a few steps and stop while the puppy is correctly beside you. Tell him to sit and give mild verbal praise. (More enthusiastic praise will encourage him to think the lesson is over.) Repeat the lesson, only increasing the number of steps you take as long as the dog is heeling nicely beside you. When you end the lesson, have him hold the sit, then give him the "Okay" to let him know that this is the end of the lesson. Praise him so that he

knows he did a good job.

The cure for excessive pulling (a common problem) is to stop when the dog is no more than 2 or 3 feet ahead of you. Guide him back into position and begin again. With a really determined puller, try switching to a head collar. This will automatically turn the pup's head toward you so you can bring him back easily to the heel position. Give quiet, reassuring praise every time the leash goes slack and he's staying with you.

Staying and heeling can take a lot out of a dog, so provide playtime and free-running exercise when the lessons are over to shake off the stress. You don't want him to associate training with all work and no fun.

STAY BY MY HEEL

To begin, step away from the dog, who is in the sit position, on your right foot. That tells the dog you aren't going anywhere. Turn and stand directly in front of him so he won't be tempted to follow. Two seconds is a long, long time to your dog, so only increase the time for which he's expected to stay in short increments. Don't force it. When practicing the heel exercise, your dog will sit at your side whenever you stop. Don't stop for more than three seconds, as your enthusiastic dog will really feel like it's an eternity!

now doesn't know if he'll get a treat or not, but he should keep performing well just in case! Finally, you will stop giving treat rewards entirely. Save them for something brand-new that you want to teach him. Keep up the praise and you'll always have a "good dog."

OBEDIENCE CLASSES

The advantages of an obedience class are that your dog will have to learn amid the distractions of other people and dogs and that your mistakes will be quickly

Practice the heel exercise in a fenced yard where there are limited distractions.

TAPERING OFF TIDBITS

Your dog has been watching you—and the hand that treats—throughout all of his lessons, and now it's time to break the treat habit. Begin by giving him treats at the end of each lesson only. Then start to give a treat after the end of only some of the lessons. At the end of every lesson, as well as during the lessons, be consistent with the praise. Your pup

DON'T STRESS ME OUT

Your dog doesn't have to deal with paying the bills, the daily commute, PTA meetings and the like, but, believe it or not, there's lots of stress in a dog's world. Stress can be caused by the owner's impatient demeanor and his angry or harsh corrections. If your dog cringes when you reach for his training collar, he's stressed. An older dog is sometimes stressed out when he goes to a new home. No matter what the cause, put off all training until he's over it. If he's going through a fear period—shying away from people, trembling when spoken to, avoiding eye contact or hiding under furniture—wait to resume training. Naturally you'd also postpone your lessons if the dog were sick, and the same goes for you. Be compassionate.

MORE PRAISE, LESS FOOD

As you progress with your puppy's lessons, and the puppy is responding well, gradually begin to treats;—weaning off in trainingwithhold the treats by alternating the treats with times when you offer only verbal praise or a few pats on the dog's side. (Pats on the head are dominant actions and he won't think they are meant to be praise.) Every lesson should end with the puppy's performing the correct action for that session's command. When he gets it right and you withhold the treat, the praise can be as long and lavish as you like. The commands are one word only, but your verbal praise can use as many words as you want...don't skimp!

corrected by the trainer. Teaching your dog along with a qualified instructor and other handlers who may have more dog experience than you are further pluses of the class environment. The instructor and other handlers can help you to find the most efficient way of teaching your dog a command or exercise. It's often easier to learn by other people's mistakes than your own. You will also learn all of the requirements for competitive obedience trials, in which you can earn titles and go on to advanced jumping and retrieving exercises, which are fun for many dogs. Obedience classes build the foundation needed for many other canine activities (in which we humans are allowed to participate, too!).

TRAINING FOR OTHER ACTIVITIES

Once your dog has basic obedience under his collar and is 12 months of age, you can enter the world of agility training. Dogs think agility is pure fun, like being turned loose in an amusement park full of obstacles! In addition to agility, there are hunting activities for sporting dogs, lure-coursing events for sighthounds, go-to-ground events for terriers, racing for the Nordic sled dogs, herding trials for the shepherd breeds and tracking, which is open to all "nosey" dogs (which would include all dogs!).

HOW DO I GET TO CARNEGIE HALL?

Or the National Obedience Championships? The same way you get your dog to do anything else—practice, practice, practice. It's how you practice that counts. Keep sessions short, varied, interesting and interspersed with active fun. A bored dog isn't learning. If you're feeling out of sorts yourself, quit for the day. Set yourself a reasonable schedule for several brief practice sessions every day and stick to it. Practice randomly throughout the day as you're doing different things around the house. Lots of praise for that good "Sit" in front of the TV or while waiting for his dinner!

For those who like to volunteer, there is the wonderful feeling of owning a Therapy Dog and visiting hospices, nursing homes and veterans' homes to bring smiles, comfort and companionship to those who live there.

Around the house, your dog can be taught to do some simple chores. You might teach him to carry a basket of household items or to fetch the morning newspaper. The kids can teach the dog all kinds of tricks, from playing hide-and-seek to balancing a biscuit on his nose. A family dog is what rounds out the family. Everything he does beyond sitting in your lap or gazing lovingly at you represents the bonus of owning a dog.

Agility trials are popular outings for Keeshonden. This Kees is clearing the bar jump with dexterity and speed.

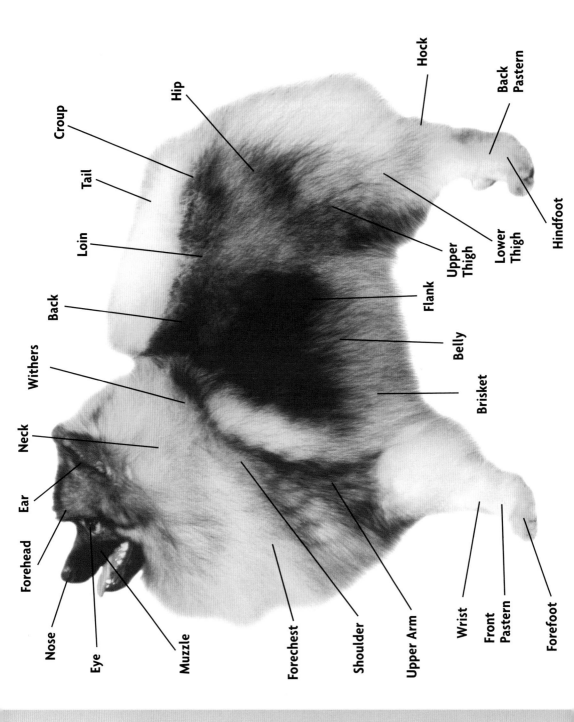

Croup

Hip

Hock

Back Pastern

Tail

Loin

Upper Thigh

Lower Thigh

Hindfoot

Back

Flank

Withers

Belly

Brisket

Neck

Ear

Forehead

Nose

Eye

Muzzle

Forechest

Shoulder

Upper Arm

Wrist

Front Pastern

Forefoot

PHYSICAL STRUCTURE OF THE KEESHOND

HEALTHCARE OF YOUR

KEESHOND

By Lowell Ackerman DVM, DACVD

HEALTHCARE FOR A LIFETIME
When you own a dog, you become his healthcare advocate over his entire lifespan, as well as being the one to shoulder the financial burden of such care. Accordingly, it is worthwhile to focus on prevention rather than treatment, as you and your pet will both be happier.

Of course, the best place to have begun your program of preventative healthcare is with the initial purchase or adoption of your dog. There is no way of guaranteeing that your new furry friend is free of medical problems, but there are some things you can do to improve your odds. You certainly should have done adequate research into the Keeshond and selected your puppy carefully rather than buying on impulse. Health issues aside, a large number of pet abandonment and relinquishment cases arise from a mismatch between pet needs and owner expectations. This is entirely preventable with appropriate planning and finding a good breeder.

Regarding healthcare issues specifically, it is very difficult to make blanket statements about where to acquire a problem-free pet, but, again, a reputable breeder is your best bet. In an ideal situation you have the opportunity to see both parents, get references from other owners of the breeder's pups and see genetic-testing documentation for several generations of the litter's ancestors. At the very least, you must thoroughly investigate your breed of interest and the problems inherent in that breed, as well as the genetic testing available to screen for those problems. Genetic testing offers some important benefits, but testing is only available for a few disorders in a relatively small number of breeds and is not available for some of the most common genetic diseases, such as hip dysplasia, cataracts, epilepsy, cardiomyopathy, etc. This area of research is indeed exciting and increasingly important, and advances will continue to be made each year. In fact, recent research has shown that there is an equivalent dog gene for 75% of known human genes, so research done in either species is

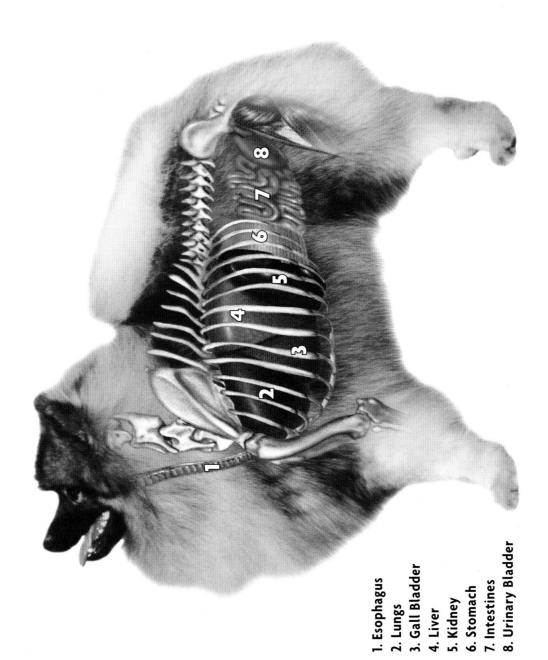

1. Esophagus
2. Lungs
3. Gall Bladder
4. Liver
5. Kidney
6. Stomach
7. Intestines
8. Urinary Bladder

INTERNAL ORGANS OF THE KEESHOND

likely to benefit the other.

We've also discussed that evaluating your chosen pup's behavioral nature and that of his immediate family members is an important part of the selection process that cannot be underestimated or underemphasized. It is sometimes difficult to evaluate temperament in puppies because certain behavioral tendencies, such as some forms of aggression, may not be immediately evident.

More dogs are euthanized each year for behavioral reasons than for all medical conditions combined, so it is critical to take temperament issues seriously. Start with a well-balanced, friendly companion and put the time and effort into proper socialization, and you will both be rewarded with a lifelong valued relationship.

With a pup from healthy, sound stock, you become responsible for helping your veterinarian keep your pet healthy. Some crucial things happen before you even bring your puppy home. Parasite control typically begins at two weeks of age, and vaccinations typically begin at six to eight weeks of age. A pre-pubertal evaluation is typically scheduled for about six months of age. At this time, a dental evaluation is done (since the adult teeth are now in), heartworm prevention is started and neutering or spaying is most commonly done.

It is critical to commence regular dental care at home if you have not already done so. It may not sound so important, but most dogs have active periodontal disease by four years of age if they don't have their teeth cleaned regularly at home, not just at their veterinary exams. Dental problems lead to more than just bad "doggie breath": gum disease can have very serious medical consequences. If you start brushing

---

TAKING YOUR DOG'S TEMPERATURE

It is important to know how to take your dog's temperature at times when you think he may be ill. It's not the most enjoyable task, but it can be done without too much difficulty. It's easier with a helper, preferably someone with whom the dog is friendly, so that one of you can hold the dog while the other inserts the thermometer.

Before inserting the thermometer, coat the end with petroleum jelly. Insert the thermometer slowly and gently into the dog's rectum about one inch. Wait for the reading, about two minutes. Be sure to remove the thermometer carefully and clean it thoroughly after each use.

A dog's normal body temperature is between 100.5 and 102.5 degrees F. Immediate veterinary attention is required if the dog's temperature is below 99 or above 104 degrees F.

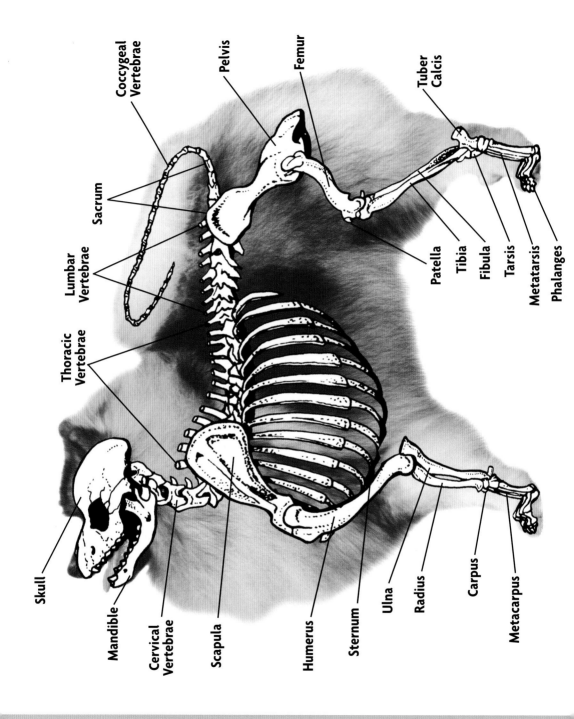

Coccygeal Vertebrae

Sacrum

Lumbar Vertebrae

Pelvis

Femur

Tuber Calcis

Patella

Tibia

Fibula

Tarsis

Metatarsis

Phalanges

Thoracic Vertebrae

Skull

Mandible

Cervical Vertebrae

Scapula

Humerus

Sternum

Ulna

Radius

Carpus

Metacarpus

SKELETAL STRUCTURE OF THE KEESHOND

your dog's teeth and using anti-septic rinses from a young age, your dog will be accustomed to it and will not resist. The results will be healthy dentition, which your pet will need to enjoy a long, healthy life.

Most dogs are considered adults at a year of age, although some larger breeds still have some filling out to do up to about two or so years old. Each breed has different healthcare requirements, so work with your veterinarian to determine what will be needed and what your role should be. This doctor-client relationship is important, because as vaccination guidelines change, there may not be an annual "vaccine visit" scheduled. You must make sure that you see your veterinarian at least annually, even if no vaccines are due, because this is the best opportunity to coordinate health-care activities and to make sure that no medical issues creep by unaddressed.

When your Keeshond reaches three-quarters of his anticipated lifespan, he is considered a "senior" and likely requires some special care. In general, if you've been taking great care of your canine companion throughout his formative and adult years, the transition to senior status should be a smooth one. Age is not a disease, and as long as everything is functioning as it should, there is no reason why most of late

adulthood should not be reward-ing for both you and your pet. This is especially true if you have tended to the details, such as regular veterinary visits, proper dental care, excellent nutrition and management of bone and joint issues.

At this stage in your dog's life, your veterinarian may want to schedule visits twice yearly, instead of once, to run some labo-ratory screenings, electrocardio-grams and the like, and to change the diet to something more digestible. Catching problems early is the best way to manage them effectively. Treating the early stages of heart disease is so much easier than trying to intervene when there is more significant damage to the heart muscle. Similarly, managing the beginning of kidney problems is fairly routine if there is no significant kidney damage. Other problems, like cognitive dysfunction (similar to senility and Alzheimer's disease), cancer, diabetes and arthritis, are more common in older dogs, but all can be treated to help the dog live as many happy, comfortable years as possi-ble. Just as in people, medical management is more effective (and less expensive) when you catch things early.

SELECTING A VETERINARIAN
There is probably no more impor-tant decision that you will make

regarding your pet's healthcare than the selection of his doctor. Your pet's veterinarian will be a pediatrician, family-practice physician and gerontologist, depending on the dog's life stage, and will be the individual who makes recommendations regarding issues such as when specialists need to be consulted, when diagnostic testing and/or therapeutic intervention is needed and when you will need to seek outside emergency and critical-care services. Your vet will act as your advocate and liaison throughout these processes.

Everyone has his own idea about what to look for in a vet, an individual who will play a big role in his dog's (and, of course, his own) life for many years to come. For some, it is the compassionate caregiver with whom they hope to develop a professional relationship to span the lifetime of their dogs and even their future pets. For others, they are seeking a clinician with keen diagnostic and therapeutic insight who can deliver state-of-the-art healthcare. Still others need a veterinary facility that is open evenings and weekends, or is in close proximity or provides mobile veterinary services, to accommodate their schedules; these people may not much mind that their dogs might

SAMPLE VACCINATION SCHEDULE

6-8 weeks of age	Parvovirus, Distemper, Adenovirus-2 (Hepatitis)
9-11 weeks of age	Parvovirus, Distemper, Adenovirus-2 (Hepatitis)
12-14 weeks of age	Parvovirus, Distemper, Adenovirus-2 (Hepatitis)
12-16 weeks of age	Rabies
1 year of age	Parvovirus, Distemper, Adenovirus-2 (Hepatitis), Rabies

Revaccination is performed every one to three years, depending on the product, the method of administration and the patient's risk. Initial adult inoculation (for dogs at least 16 weeks of age in which a puppy series was not done or could not be confirmed) is two vaccinations, done three to four weeks apart, with revaccination according to the same criteria mentioned. Other vaccines are given as decided between owner and veterinarian.

see different veterinarians on each visit. Just as we have different reasons for selecting our own healthcare professionals (e.g., covered by insurance plan, expert in field, convenient location, etc.), we should not expect that there is a one-size-fits-all recommendation for selecting a veterinarian and veterinary practice. The best advice is to be honest in your assessment of what you expect from a veterinary practice and to conscientiously research the options in your area. You will quickly appreciate that not all veterinary practices are the same and you will be happiest with one that truly meets your needs.

There is another point to be considered in the selection of veterinary services. Not that long ago, a single veterinarian would attempt to manage all medical and surgical issues as they arose. That was often problematic, because veterinarians are trained in many species and many diseases, and it was just impossible for general veterinary practitioners to be experts in every species, every field and every ailment. However, just as in the human healthcare fields, specialization has allowed general practitioners to concentrate on primary healthcare delivery, especially wellness and the prevention of infectious diseases, and to utilize a network of specialists to assist in the management of conditions that require

YOUR DOG NEEDS TO VISIT THE VET IF:
- He has ingested a toxin such as antifreeze or a toxic plant; in these cases, administer first aid and call the vet right away
- His teeth are discolored, loose or missing or he has sores and/or other signs of infection or abnormality in the mouth
- He has been vomiting, has had diarrhea or has been constipated for over 24 hours; call immediately if you notice blood in his stool
- He has refused food for over 24 hours
- His eating habits, water intake and/or toilet habits have become subject to a noticeable degree of change; you have noticed weight gain or weight loss
- He shows symptoms of bloat, , which require immediate attention
- He is salivating excessively
- He has a lump in his throat
- He has a lumps or bumps anywhere on the body
- He is very lethargic
- He appears to be in pain or otherwise has trouble chewing or swallowing
- His skin loses elasticity.

Of course, there will be other instances in which a visit to the vet is necessary; these are just some of the signs that could be indicative of serious problems that need to be caught as early as possible.

specific expertise and experience. Thus there are now many types of veterinary specialists, including dermatologists, cardiologists, ophthalmologists, surgeons, internists, oncologists, neurologists, behaviorists, criticalists and others to help primary-care veterinarians deal with complicated medical challenges. In most cases, specialists see cases referred by primary-care veterinarians, make diagnoses and set up management plans. From there, the animals' ongoing care is returned to their primary-care veterinarians. This important team approach to your pet's medical-care needs has provided opportunities for advanced care and an unparalleled level of quality to be delivered.

With all of the opportunities for your Keeshond to receive high-quality veterinary medical care, there is another topic that needs to be addressed at the same time—cost. It's been said that you can have excellent healthcare or inexpensive healthcare, but never both; this is as true in veterinary medicine as it is in human medicine. While veterinary costs are a fraction of what the same services cost in the human healthcare arena, it is still difficult to deal with unanticipated medical costs, especially since they can easily creep into hundreds or even thousands of dollars if specialists or emergency services become

involved. However, there are ways of managing these risks. The easiest is to buy pet health insurance and realize that its foremost purpose is not to cover routine healthcare visits but rather to serve as an umbrella for those rainy days when your pet needs medical care and you don't want to worry about whether or not you can afford that care.

Pet insurance policies are very cost-effective (and very inexpensive by human health-insurance standards), but make sure that you buy the policy long before you intend to use it (preferably starting in puppyhood, because coverage will exclude pre-existing conditions) and that you are actually buying an indemnity insurance plan from an insurance company that is regulated by your state or province. Many insurance policy look-alikes are actually discount clubs that are only redeemable at specific locations and for specific services. An indemnity plan covers your pet at almost all veterinary, specialty and emergency practices and is an excellent way to manage your pet's ongoing healthcare needs.

VACCINATIONS AND INFECTIOUS DISEASES

There has never been an easier time to prevent a variety of infectious diseases in your dog, but these advances come with a price—choice. Now, while it may seem that choice is a good thing (and it is), it has never been more difficult for the pet owner (or the veterinarian) to make an informed decision about the best way to protect pets through vaccination.

Years ago, it was just accepted that puppies got a starter series of vaccinations and then annual "boosters" throughout their lives to keep them protected. As more and more vaccines became available, consumers wanted the convenience of having all of that protection in a single injection. The result was "multivalent"

vaccines that crammed a lot of protection into a single syringe. The manufacturers' recommendations were to give the vaccines annually, and this was a simple enough protocol to follow. However, as veterinary medicine has become more sophisticated and we have started looking more at healthcare quandaries rather than convenience, it became necessary to reevaluate the situation and deal with some tough questions. It is important to realize that whether or not to use a particular vaccine depends on the

DISEASE REFERENCE CHART

	WHAT IS IT?	WHAT CAUSES IT?	SYMPTOMS
Leptospirosis	Severe disease that affects the internal organs; can be spread to people.	A bacterium, which is often carried by rodents, that enters through mucous membranes and spreads quickly throughout the body.	Range from fever, vomiting and loss of appetite in less severe cases to shock, irreversible kidney damage and possibly death in most severe cases.
Rabies	Potentially deadly virus that infects warm-blooded mammals.	Bite from a carrier of the virus, mainly wild animals.	1st stage: dog exhibits change in behavior, fear. 2nd stage: dog's behavior becomes more aggressive. 3rd stage: loss of coordination, trouble with bodily functions.
Parvovirus	Highly contagious virus, potentially deadly.	Ingestion of the virus, which is usually spread through the feces of infected dogs.	Most common: severe diarrhea. Also vomiting, fatigue, lack of appetite.
Canine cough	Contagious respiratory infection.	Combination of types of bacteria and virus. Most common: *Bordetella bronchiseptica* bacteria and parainfluenza virus.	Chronic cough.
Distemper	Disease primarily affecting respiratory and nervous system.	Virus that is related to the human measles virus.	Mild symptoms such as fever, lack of appetite and mucus secretion progress to evidence of brain damage, "hard pad."
Hepatitis	Virus primarily affecting the liver.	Canine adenovirus type I (CAV-I). Enters system when dog breathes in particles.	Lesser symptoms include listlessness, diarrhea, vomiting. More severe symptoms include "blue-eye" (clumps of virus in eye).
Coronavirus	Virus resulting in digestive problems.	Virus is spread through infected dog's feces.	Stomach upset evidenced by lack of appetite, vomiting, diarrhea.

risk of contracting the disease against which it protects, the severity of the disease if it is contracted, the duration of immunity provided by the vaccine, the safety of the product and the needs of the individual animal. In a very general sense, rabies, distemper, hepatitis and parvovirus are considered core vaccine needs, while parainfluenza, *Bordetella bronchiseptica*, Leptospirosis, coronavirus and borreliosis (Lyme disease) are considered non-core needs and best reserved for animals that demonstrate reasonable risk of contracting the diseases.

THE GREAT VACCINATION DEBATE
What kinds of questions need to be addressed? When the vet injects multiple organisms at the

same time, might some of the components interfere with one another in the development of immunologic protection? We don't have the comprehensive answer for that question, but it does appear that the immune system better handles agents when given individually. Unfortunately, most manufacturers still bundle their vaccine components because that is what most pet owners want, so getting vaccines with single components can sometimes be difficult.

Another question has to do with how often vaccines should be given. Again, this seems to be different for each vaccine component. There seems to be a general consensus that a puppy (or a dog with an unknown vaccination history) should get a series of vaccinations to initially stimulate his immunity and then a booster at one year of age, but, after that, even the veterinary associations and colleges have trouble reaching agreement. Rabies vaccination schedules are not debated, because vaccine schedules for this contagious and devastating disease are determined by government agencies. Regarding the rest, some recommend that we continue to give the vaccines annually because this method has worked well as a disease preventative for decades and delivers predictable protection. Others

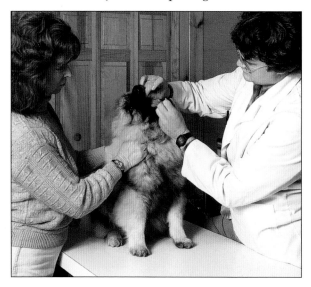

Your Keeshond's veterinary examination should be thorough, from head to toe.

recommend that some of the vaccines only need to be given every second or third year, as this can be done without affecting levels of protection. This is probably true for some vaccine components (such as hepatitis), but there have been no large studies to demonstrate what the optimal interval should be and whether the same principles hold true for all breeds.

It may be best to just measure titers, which are protective blood levels of various vaccine components, on an annual basis, but that too is not without controversy. Scientists have not precisely determined the minimum titer of specific vaccine components that will be guaranteed to provide a pet with protection. Pets with very high titers will clearly be protected and those with very low titers will need repeat vaccinations, but there is also a large "gray zone" of pets that probably have intermediate protection and may or may not need repeat vaccination, depending on their risk of coming in contact with the disease.

These questions leave primary-care veterinarians in a very uncomfortable position, one that is not easy to resolve. Do they recommend annual vaccination in a manner that has demonstrated successful protection for decades, do they recommend skipping vaccines some years and hope

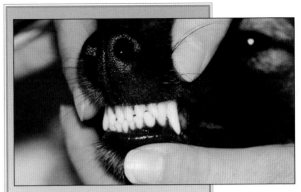

DOGGIE DENTAL DON'TS

A veterinary dental exam is necessary if you notice one or any combination of the following in your dog:
- Broken, loose or missing teeth
- Loss of appetite (which could be due to mouth pain or illness caused by infection)
- Gum abnormalities, including redness, swelling and/or bleeding
- Drooling, with or without blood
- Yellowing of the teeth and/or gumline, indicating tartar
- Bad breath.

that the protection lasts or do they measure blood tests (titers) and hope that the results are convincing enough to clearly indicate whether repeat vaccination is warranted?

These aren't the only vaccination questions impacting pets, owners and veterinarians. Other controversies focus on whether vaccines should be dosed according to body weight (currently they are administered in uniform doses, regardless of the animal's size), whether there are breed-specific issues important in determining vaccination programs (for instance, we know that some breeds have a harder time mounting an appropriate immune response to parvovirus vaccine and might benefit from a different dose or injection interval) and which type of vaccine—live-virus or inactivated—offers more advantages with fewer disadvantages. Clearly, there are many more questions than there are answers. The important thing, as a pet owner, is to be aware of the issues and be able to work with your veterinarian to make decisions that are right for your pet. Be an informed consumer and you will appreciate the deliberation required in tailoring a vaccination program to best meet the needs of your pet. Expect also that this is an ongoing, ever-changing topic of debate; thus, the decisions you make this year won't necessarily be the same as the ones you make next year.

COMMON VACCINATIONS
Now that you are more confused than ever about vaccination, it is a good time to discuss some of the diseases that create the need for vaccination in the first place. Following are the major canine infectious diseases and a simple explanation of each.

Rabies is a devastating viral disease that can be fatal in dogs and people. In fact, vaccination of dogs and cats is an important public-health measure to create a resistant animal buffer population to protect people from contracting the disease. Vaccination schedules are determined on a government level and are not optional for pet owners; rabies vaccination is required by law in all 50 states.

Parvovirus is a severe, potentially life-threatening disease that is easily transmitted between dogs. There are four strains of the virus, but it is believed that there is significant "cross-protection" between strains that may be included in individual vaccines.

Distemper is another potentially severe and life-threatening disease with a relatively high risk of exposure, especially in certain regions. In very high-risk distemper environments, young pups may be vaccinated with human measles vaccine, a related virus that offers cross-protection when administered at 4-10 weeks of age.

Hepatitis is caused by canine adenovirus type 1 (CAV-1), but since vaccination with the causative virus has a higher rate of adverse effects, cross-protection is derived from the use of adenovirus type 2 (CAV-2), a cause of respiratory disease and one of the potential causes of canine cough. Vaccination with CAV-2 provides long-term immunity against hepatitis, but relatively less protection against respiratory infection.

Canine cough (tracheobronchitis) is actually a fairly complicated result of viral and bacterial offenders; therefore, even with vaccination, protection is incomplete. Wherever dogs congregate, canine cough will likely be spread among them. Intranasal vaccination with *Bordetella* and parainfluenza is the best safeguard, but the duration of immunity does not appear to be very long, typically a year at most. These are non-core vaccines, but vaccination is sometimes mandated by boarding kennels, obedience classes, dog shows and other places where dogs congregate to try to minimize spread of infection.

Leptospirosis is a potentially fatal disease that is more common in some geographic regions. It is capable of being spread to humans. The disease varies with the individual "serovar," or strain, of Leptospira involved; since there does not appear to be much cross-protection between serovars, protection is only as good as the likelihood that the serovar in the vaccine is the same as the one in the pet's local environment. Problems with *Leptospira* vaccines are that protection does not last very long, side effects are not uncommon and a large percentage of dogs (perhaps 30%) may not respond to vaccination.

FOAMING DOGS: PASTEUR TO THE RESCUE

Rabies, as old as any plague, dates back to Babylonian days, the 23rd century BC. The term may derive from the Sanskrit word "rabhas," which translates to "to do violence." In the 16th century, Girolama Fracastoro was the first scientist to describe the disease, which he did some 350 years prior to Louis Pasteur, the scientist well known is his day for "pasteurizing" milk and beer.

In the 1870s, Pasteur emerged as a much-needed savior from terror in an irrational world. Ironically, his first effort in dealing with human disease was a vaccine for anthrax, which, like rabies, affects humans and animals alike. Rabies scourged Europe with a vengeance, and victims of the "violent virus" were either killed or committed suicide. Pasteur developed a vaccine for rabies by injecting brain material from a rabid dog into the bloodstream of a healthy dog. Once he developed a way of adjusting the virulence of the inoculation, he could build up the animal's resistance to the disease through a series of stronger inoculations. Since the virus developed slowly in an affected dog, it was able to develop immunity to the rabies before the incubation period had ended. After much experimentation, Pasteur was able to treat humans and, in 1885, his remarkable vaccination saved the first of millions of human beings.

Borrelia burgdorferi is the cause of Lyme disease, the risk of which varies with the geographic area in which the pet lives and travels. Lyme disease is spread by deer ticks in the eastern US and western black-legged ticks in the western part of the country, and the risk of exposure is high in some regions. Lameness, fever and inappetence are most commonly seen in affected dogs. The extent of protection from the vaccine has not been conclusively demonstrated.

Coronavirus has a high risk of exposure, especially in areas where dogs congregate, but it typically causes only mild to moderate digestive upset (diarrhea, vomiting, etc.). Vaccines are available, but the duration of protection is believed to be relatively short and the effectiveness of the vaccine in preventing infection is considered low.

There are many other vaccinations available, including those for *Giardia* and canine adenovirus-1. While there may be some specific indications for their use, and local risk factors to be considered, they are not widely recommended for most dogs.

NEUTERING/SPAYING

Sterilization procedures (neutering for males/spaying for females) are meant to accomplish several purposes. While the underlying premise is to address the risk of pet overpopulation, there are also some medical and behavioral benefits to the surgeries as well. For females, spaying prior to the first estrus (heat cycle) leads to a marked reduction in the risk of mammary cancer. There are also no manifestations of "heat" to

PSEUDOPREGNANCY

Pseudopregnancy in female dogs is proof that dogs can delude themselves the same way people can—maybe moreso. Your female dog can experience a pseudopregnancy if she is not bred during her estrous cycle. This pseudocyesis usually occurs about eight weeks after her period and is accompanied by swollen mammary glands and an enlarged abdomen. Your bitch may "adopt" one of her toys as her litter and demonstrate nesting behavior (digging a burrow in your couch or her bed). She may also exhibit aggressive behavior toward humans who attempt to threaten her "litter."

Pseudocyesis may trace back to wolf behavior in the wild. Commonly the aunts or granddam of a litter will assist another bitch in her pack with her litter. All of the bitches will feed the pups and protect them.

Since there are health risks involved with pseudopregnancy, owners are advised to spay their bitches to prevent a recurrence. Bitches can suffer from uterine infections, which can threaten their lives.

attract male dogs and no bleeding in the house. For males, there is prevention of testicular cancer and a reduction in the risk of prostate problems. In both sexes, there may be some limited reduction in aggressive behaviors toward other dogs, and some diminishing of urine marking, roaming and mounting.

While neutering and spaying do indeed prevent animals from contributing to pet overpopulation, even no-cost and low-cost neutering options have not eliminated the problem. Perhaps one of the main reasons for this is that individuals that intentionally breed their dogs and those that allow their animals to run at large are the main causes of unwanted offspring. Also, animals in shelters are often there because they were abandoned or relinquished, not because they came from unplanned matings. Neutering/spaying is important, but it should be considered in the context of the real causes of animals' ending up in shelters and eventually being euthanized.

One of the important considerations regarding neutering is that it is a surgical procedure. This sometimes gets lost in discussions of low-cost procedures and commoditization of the process. In females, spaying is specifically referred to as an ovariohysterectomy. In this procedure, a midline incision is made in the abdomen and the entire uterus and both ovaries are surgically removed. While this is a major invasive surgical procedure, it usually has few complications because it is typically performed on young healthy animals. However, it is a major surgery, as any woman who has had a hysterectomy will attest.

In males, neutering has traditionally referred to castration, which involves the surgical removal of both testicles. While still a significant piece of surgery, there is not the abdominal exposure that is required in the female surgery. In addition, there is now a chemical sterilization option, in which a solution is injected into each testicle, leading to atrophy of the sperm-producing cells. This can typically be done under sedation rather than full anesthesia. This is a relatively new approach, and there are no long-term clinical studies yet available.

Neutering/spaying is typically done around six months of age at most veterinary hospitals, although techniques have been pioneered to perform the procedures in animals as young as eight weeks of age. In general, the surgeries on the very young animals are done for the specific reason of sterilizing them before they go to their new homes. This is done in some shelter hospitals for assurance that the animals will definitely not produce any pups. Otherwise, these organizations need to rely on owners to comply with their wishes to have the animals "altered" at a later date, something that does not always happen.

There are some exciting immunocontraceptive "vaccines" currently under development, and there may be a time when contraception in pets will not require surgical procedures. We anxiously await these developments.

HIT ME WITH A HOT SPOT

What is a hot spot? Technically known as pyotraumatic dermatitis, a hot spot is an infection on the dog's coat, usually by the rear end, under the tail or on a leg, which the dog inflicts upon himself. The dog licks and bites the itchy spot until it becomes inflamed and infected. The hot spot can range in size from the circumference of a grape to the circumference of an apple. Provided that the hot spot is not related to a deeper bacterial infection, it can be treated topically by clipping the area, cleaning the sore and giving prednisone. For bacterial infections, antibiotics are required. In some cases, an Elizabethan collar is required to keep the dog from further irritating the hot spot. The itching can intensify and the pain becomes worse. Medicated shampoos and cool compresses, drying agents and topical steroids may be prescribed by your vet as well.

Hot spots can be caused by fleas, an allergy, an ear infection, anal sac problems, mange or a foreign irritant. Likewise, they can be linked to psychoses. The underlying problem must be addressed in addition to the hot spot. Generally, dogs with heavier coats are more prone to hot spots than short-coated breeds.

Recognizing a Sick Dog

Unlike colicky babies and cranky children, our canine kids cannot tell us when they are feeling ill. However, there are a number of signs that owners can identify to know that their dogs are not feeling well.

Take note of physical manifestations such as:

- unusual bad odor, including bad breath
- excessive shedding
- wax in the ears, chronic ear irritation
- oily, flaky, dull haircoat
- mucus, tearing or similar discharge in the eyes
- fleas or mites
- mucus in stool, diarrhea
- sensitivity to petting or handling
- licking at paws, scratching face, etc.

Keep an eye out for behavioral changes as well including:

- lethargy, idleness
- lack of patience or general irritability
- lack of interest in food
- phobias (fear of people, loud noises, etc.)
- strange behavior, suspicion, fear
- coprophagia
- more frequent barking
- whimpering, crying

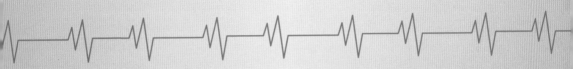

Get Well Soon

You don't need a DVM to provide good TLC to your sick or recovering dog, but you do need to pay attention to some details that normally wouldn't bother him. The following tips will aid Fido's recovery and get him back on his paws again:

- Keep his space free of irritating smells, like heavy perfumes and air fresheners.
- Rest is the best medicine! Avoid harsh lighting that will prevent your dog from sleeping. Shade him from bright sunlight during the day and dim the lights in the evening.
- Keep the noise level down. Animals are more sensitive to sound when they are sick.

- Be attentive to any necessary temperature adjustments. A dog with a fever needs a cool room and cold liquids. A bitch that is whelping or recovering from surgery will be more comfortable in a warm room, consuming warm liquids and food.
- You wouldn't send a sick child back to school early, so don't rush your dog back into a full routine until he seems absolutely ready.

S. E. M. BY DR. DENNIS KUNKEL, UNIVERSITY OF HAWAII.

A scanning electron micrograph of a dog flea, *Ctenocephalides canis*, on dog hair.

EXTERNAL PARASITES

FLEAS

Fleas have been around for millions of years and, while we have better tools now for controlling them than at any time in the past, there still is little chance that they will end up on an endangered species list. Actually, they are very well adapted to living on our pets, and they continue to adapt as we make advances.

The female flea can consume 15 times her weight in blood during active reproduction and can lay as many as 40 eggs a day. These eggs are very resistant to the effects of insecticides. They hatch into larvae, which then mature and spin cocoons. The immature fleas reside in this pupal stage until the time is right for feeding. This pupal stage is also very resistant to the effects of insecticides, and pupae can last in the environment without feeding for many months. Newly emergent fleas are attracted to animals by the warmth of the animals' bodies, movement and exhaled carbon dioxide. However, when they first emerge from their cocoons, they orient towards light; thus, when an animal passes between a flea and the light source, casting a shadow, the flea pounces and starts to feed. If the animal turns out to be a dog or cat, the reproductive cycle continues. If the flea lands on another type of animal, including a person, the flea will bite but will then look for a more appropriate host. An emerging adult flea can survive without feeding for up to 12 months but, once it tastes blood, it can only survive off its host for three to four days.

It was once thought that fleas spend most of their lives in the environment, but we now know that fleas won't willingly jump off a dog unless leaping to another dog or when physically removed by brushing, bathing or other manipulation. Flea eggs, on the other hand, are shiny and smooth, and they roll off the animal and into the environment. The eggs, larvae and pupae then exist in the environment, but once the adult finds a susceptible animal, it's home sweet home until the flea is convinced to seek refuge elsewhere.

Since adult fleas live on the animal and immature forms survive in the environment, a successful treatment plan must address all stages of the flea life cycle. There are now several safe and effective flea-control products that can be applied on a monthly

---

FLEA PREVENTION FOR YOUR DOG

- Discuss with your veterinarian the safest product to protect your dog, likely in the form of a monthly tablet or a liquid preparation placed on the back of the dog's neck.
- For dogs suffering from flea-bite dermatitis, a shampoo or topical insecticide treatment is required.
- Your lawn and property should be sprayed with an insecticide designed to kill fleas and ticks that lurk outdoors.
- Using a flea comb, check the dog's coat regularly for any signs of parasites.
- Practice good housekeeping: vacuum floors, carpets and furniture regularly, especially in the areas that the dog frequents, and wash the dog's bedding weekly.
- Follow up house-cleaning with carpet shampoos and sprays to rid the house of fleas at all stages of development. Insect growth regulators are the safest option.

---

basis. These include fipronil, imidacloprid, selamectin and permethrin (found in several formulations). Most of these products have significant flea-killing rates within 24 hours. However, none of them will control the immature forms in the environment. To accomplish this, there are a variety of insect growth regulators that can be

THE FLEA'S LIFE CYCLE

What came first, the flea or the egg? This age-old mystery is more difficult to comprehend than the actual cycle of the flea. Fleas usually live only about four months. A female can lay 2,000 eggs in her lifetime.

Photo by Carolina Biological Supply Co.

Egg

After ten days of rolling around your carpet or under your furniture, the eggs hatch into larvae, which feed on various and sundry debris. In days or months, depending on the climate, the larvae spin a cocoon and develop into the pupal or nymph stage, which quickly develop into fleas.

Photo by Carolina Biological Supply Co.

Larva

Pupa

These immature fleas must locate a host within 10 to 14 days or they will die. Only about 1% of the flea population exist as adult fleas, while the other 99% exist as eggs, larvae or pupae.

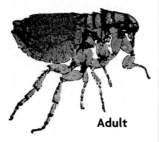

Adult

KILL FLEAS THE NATURAL WAY

If you choose not to go the route of conventional medication, there are some natural ways to ward off fleas:

- Dust your dog with a natural flea powder, composed of such herbal goodies as rosemary, wormwood, pennyroyal, citronella, rue, tobacco powder and eucalyptus.
- Apply diatomaceous earth, the fossilized remains of single-cell algae, to your carpets, furniture and pet's bedding. Even though it's not good for dogs, it's even worse for fleas, which will dry up swiftly and die.
- Brush your dog frequently, give him adequate exercise and let him fast occasionally. All of these activities strengthen the dog's system and make him more resistant to disease and parasites.
- Bathe your dog with a capful of pennyroyal or eucalyptus oil.
- Feed a natural diet, free of additives and preservatives. Add some fresh garlic and brewer's yeast to the dog's morning portion, as these items have flea-repelling properties.

sprayed into the environment (e.g., pyriproxyfen, methoprene, fenoxycarb) as well as insect development inhibitors such as lufenuron that can be administered. These compounds have no effect on adult fleas, but they stop immature forms from developing into adults. In years gone by, we relied heavily on toxic insecticides (such as organophosphates, organochlorines and carbamates) to manage the flea problem, but today's options are not only much safer to use on our pets but also safer for the environment.

TICKS

Ticks are members of the spider class (arachnids) and are blood-sucking parasites capable of transmitting a variety of diseases, including Lyme disease, ehrlichiosis, babesiosis and Rocky Mountain spotted fever. It's easy to see ticks on your own skin, but it is more of a challenge when your furry companion is affected. Whenever you happen to be planning a stroll in a tick-infested area (especially forests, grassy or wooded areas or parks) be prepared to do a thorough inspection of your dog afterward to search for ticks. Ticks can be tricky, so make sure you spend time looking in the ears, between the toes and everywhere else where a tick might hide. Ticks need to be attached for 24–72 hours before they transmit most of the diseases that they carry, so you do have a window of opportunity for some preventative intervention.

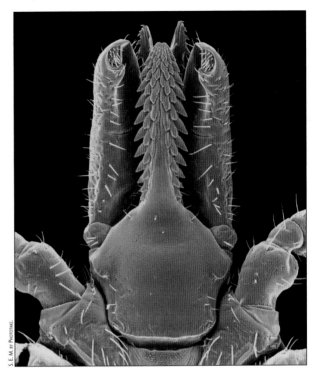

S. E. M. BY PHOTOTAKE.

A scanning electron micrograph of the head of a female deer tick, *Ixodes dammini*, a parasitic tick that carries Lyme disease.

A TICKING BOMB

There is nothing good about a tick's harpooning his nose into your dog's skin. Among the diseases caused by ticks are Rocky Mountain spotted fever, canine ehrlichiosis, canine babesiosis, canine hepatozoonosis and Lyme disease. If a dog is allergic to the saliva of a female wood tick, he can develop tick paralysis.

Female ticks live to eat and breed. They can lay between 4,000 and 5,000 eggs and they die soon after. Males, on the other hand, live only to mate with the females and continue the process as long as they are able. Most ticks live on multiple hosts before parasitizing dogs. The immature forms typically reside on grass and shrubs, waiting for susceptible animals to walk by. The larvae and nymph stages typically feed on wildlife.

If only a few ticks are present on a dog, they can be plucked out, but it is important to remove the entire head and mouthparts,

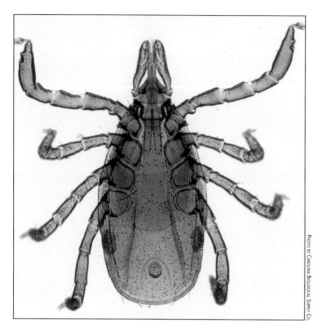

Photo by Carolina Biological Supply Co.

Deer tick,
Ixodes dammini.

disposed of in a container of alcohol or flushed down the toilet.

Some of the newer flea products, specifically those with fipronil, selamectin and permethrin, have effect against some, but not all, species of tick. Flea collars containing appropriate insecticides (e.g., propoxur, chlorfenvinphos) can aid in tick control. In most areas, such collars should be placed on animals in March, at the beginning of the tick season, and changed regularly. Leaving the collar on when the insecticide level is waning invites the development of resistance. Amitraz collars are also good for tick control, and the active ingredient does not interfere with other flea-control products. The ingredient helps prevent the attachment of ticks to the skin and will cause those ticks already on the skin to detach themselves.

which may be deeply embedded in the skin. This is best accomplished with forceps designed especially for this purpose; fingers can be used but should be protected with rubber gloves, plastic wrap or at least a paper towel. The tick should be grasped as closely as possible to the animal's skin and should be pulled upward with steady, even pressure. Do not squeeze, crush or puncture the body of the tick or you risk exposure to any disease carried by that tick. Once the ticks have been removed, the sites of attachment should be disinfected. Your hands should then be washed with soap and water to further minimize risk of contagion. The tick should be

TICK CONTROL

Removal of underbrush and leaf litter and the thinning of trees in areas where tick control is desired are recommended. These actions remove the cover and food sources for small animals that serve as hosts for ticks. With continued mowing of grasses in these areas, the probability of ticks' surviving is further reduced. A variety of insecticide ingredients (e.g., resmethrin, carbaryl, permethrin, chlorpyrifos, dioxathion and allethrin) are registered for tick control around the home.

MITES

Mites are tiny arachnid parasites that parasitize the skin of dogs. Skin diseases caused by mites are referred to as "mange," and there are many different forms seen in dogs. These forms are very different from one another, each one warranting an individual description.

Sarcoptic mange, or scabies, is one of the itchiest conditions that affects dogs. The microscopic *Sarcoptes* mites burrow into the superficial layers of the skin and can drive dogs crazy with itchiness. They are also communicable to people, although they can't complete their reproductive cycle on people. Not only are the mites tiny but also are often difficult to find when trying to make a diagnosis. Skin scrapings from multiple areas are examined microscopically but, even then, sometimes the mites cannot be found.

Fortunately, scabies is relatively easy to treat, and there are a variety of products that will successfully kill the mites. Since the mites can't live in the environment for very long without feeding, a complete cure is usually possible within four to eight weeks.

Cheyletiellosis is caused by a relatively large mite, which sometimes can be seen even without a microscope. Often referred to as "walking dandruff," this also causes itching, but not usually as profound as with scabies.

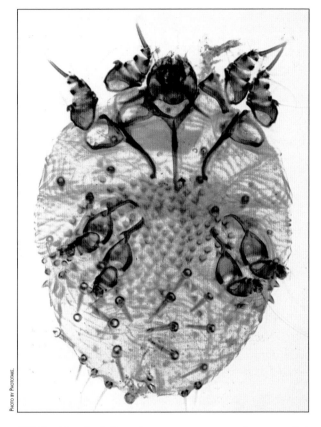

PHOTO BY PHOTOTAKE.

Sarcoptes scabiei, commonly known as the "itch mite."

While *Cheyletiella* mites can survive somewhat longer in the environment than scabies mites, they too are relatively easy to treat, being responsive not only to the medications used to treat scabies but also often to flea-control products.

Otodectes cynotis is the cause of ear mites and is one of the more common causes of mange, especially in young dogs in shelters or pet stores. That's because the mites are typically present in large numbers and are quickly spread to

Micrograph of a dog louse, *Heterodoxus spiniger*. Female lice attach their eggs to the hairs of the dog. As the eggs hatch, the larval lice bite and feed on the blood. Lice can also feed on dead skin and hair. This feeding activity can cause hair loss and skin problems.

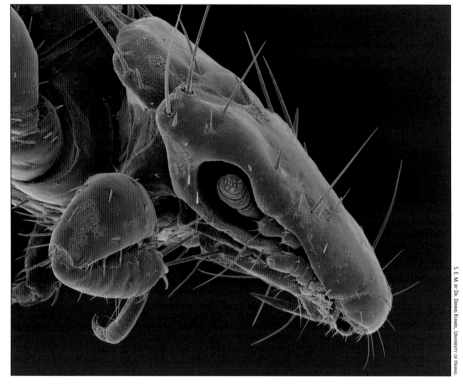

S. E. M. BY DR. DENNIS KUNKEL, UNIVERSITY OF HAWAII

nearby animals. The mites rarely do much harm, but can be difficult to eradicate if the treatment regimen is not comprehensive. While many try to treat the condition with ear drops only, this is the most common cause of treatment failure. Ear drops cause the mites to simply move out of the ears and as far away as possible (usually to the base of the tail) until the insecticide levels in the ears drop to an acceptable level—then it's back to business as usual! The successful treatment of ear mites requires treating all animals in the household with a systemic insecticide, such as selamectin, or a combination of miticidal ear drops combined with whole-body flea-control preparations.

Demodicosis, sometimes referred to as red mange, can be one of the most difficult forms of mange to treat. Part of the problem has to do with the fact that the mites live in the hair follicles and are relatively well shielded from topical and systemic products. The main issue, however, is that demodectic mange typically only results when there is some underlying process interfering with the dog's immune system.

Since *Demodex* mites are normal residents of the skin of

mammals, including humans, there is usually only a mite population explosion when the immune system fails to keep the number of mites in check. In young animals, the immune deficit may be transient or may reflect an actual inherited immune problem. In older animals, demodicosis is usually seen only when there is another disease hampering the immune system, such as diabetes, cancer, thyroid problems or the use of immune-suppressing drugs. Accordingly, treatment involves not only trying to kill the mange mites but also discerning what is interfering with immune function and correcting it if possible.

Chiggers represent several different species of mite that don't parasitize dogs specifically, but do latch on to passersby and can cause irritation. The problem is most prevalent in wooded areas in the late summer and fall. Treatment is not difficult, as the mites do not complete their life cycle on dogs and are susceptible to a variety of insecticides.

MOSQUITOES

Mosquitoes have long been known to transmit a variety of diseases to people, as well as just being biting pests during warm weather. They also pose a real risk to pets. Not only do they carry deadly heartworms but

recently there also has been much concern over their involvement with West Nile virus. While we can avoid heartworm with the use of preventive medications, there are no such preventives for West Nile virus. The only method of prevention in endemic areas is active mosquito control. Fortunately, most dogs that have been exposed to the virus only developed flu-like symptoms and, to date, there have not been the large number of reported deaths in canines as seen in some other species.

Illustration of *Demodex folliculoram*.

ILLUSTRATION BY PHOTOTAKE.

MOSQUITO REPELLENT

Low concentrations of DEET (less than 10%), found in many human mosquito repellents, have been safely used in dogs but, in these concentrations, probably give only about two hours of protection. DEET may be safe in these small concentrations, but since it is not licensed for use on dogs, there is no research proving its safety for dogs. Products containing permethrin give the longest-lasting protection, perhaps two to four weeks. As DEET is not licensed for use on dogs, and both DEET and permethrin can be quite toxic to cats, appropriate care should be exercised. Other products, such as those containing oil of citronella, also have some mosquito-repellent activity but typically have a relatively short duration of action.

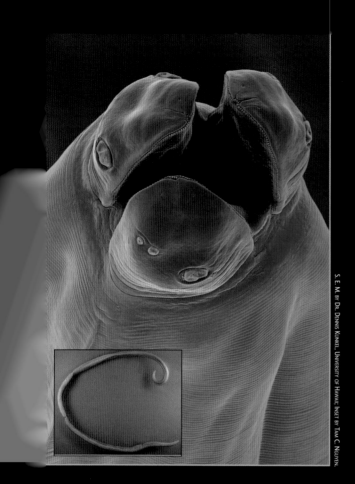

S. E. M. BY DR. DENNIS KUNKEL, UNIVERSITY OF HAWAII; INSET BY TAM C. NGUYEN.

The ascarid roundworm *Toxocara canis*, showing the mouth with three lips. Inset: photomicrograph of the roundworm *Ascaris lumbricoides*.

INTERNAL PARASITES: WORMS

ASCARIDS

Ascarids are intestinal roundworms that rarely cause severe disease in dogs. Nonetheless, they are of major public health significance because they can be transferred to people. Sadly, it is children who are most commonly affected by the parasite, probably from inadvertently ingesting ascarid-contaminated soil. In fact, many yards and children's sandboxes contain appreciable numbers of ascarid eggs. So, while ascarids don't bite dogs or latch onto their intestines to suck blood, they do cause some nasty medical conditions in children and are best eradicated from our furry friends. Because pups can start passing ascarid eggs by three weeks of age, most parasite-control programs begin at two weeks of age and are repeated every two weeks until pups are eight weeks old. It is important to

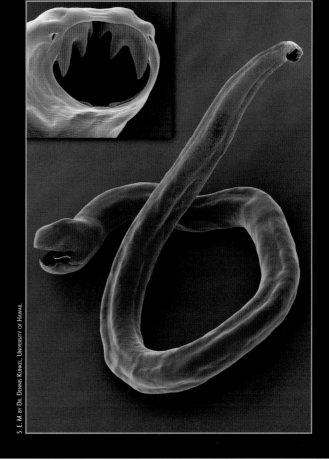

S. E. M BY DR. DENNIS KUNKEL, UNIVERSITY OF HAWAII.

realize that bitches can pass ascarids to their pups even if they test negative prior to whelping. Accordingly, bitches are best treated at the same time as the pups.

HOOKWORMS

Unlike ascarids, hookworms do latch onto a dog's intestinal tract and can cause significant loss of blood and protein. Similar to ascarids, hookworms can be transmitted to humans, where they cause a condition known as cutaneous larval migrans. Dogs can become infected either by consuming the infective larvae or by the larvae's penetrating the skin directly. People most often get infected when they are lying on the ground (such as on a beach) and the larvae penetrate the skin. Yes, the larvae can penetrate through a beach blanket. Hookworms are typically susceptible to the same medications used to treat ascarids.

The hookworm *Ancylostoma caninum* infects the colon of dogs. Inset: Note the row of hooks at the posterior end, used to anchor the worm to the intestinal wall.

WHIPWORMS

Whipworms latch onto the lower aspects of the dog's colon and can cause cramping and diarrhea. Eggs do not start to appear in the dog's feces until about three months after the dog was infected. This worm has a peculiar life cycle, which makes it more difficult to control than ascarids or hookworms. The good thing is that whipworms rarely are transferred to people.

Some of the medications used to treat ascarids and hookworms are also effective against whipworms, but, in general, a separate treatment protocol is needed. Since most of the medications are effective against the adults but not the eggs or larvae, treatment is typically repeated in three weeks,

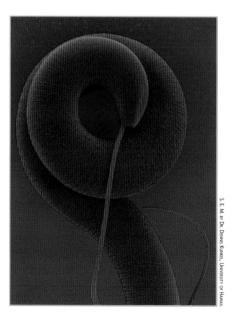

Adult whipworm, *Trichuris* sp., an intestinal parasite.

S. E. M. BY DR. DENNIS KUNKEL, UNIVERSITY OF HAWAII.

> ## WORM CONTROL GUIDELINES
> - Practice sanitary habits with your dog and home.
> - Clean up after your dog and don't let him sniff or eat other dogs' droppings.
> - Control insects and fleas in the dog's environment. Fleas, lice, cockroaches, beetles, mice and rats can act as hosts for various worms.
> - Prevent dogs from eating uncooked meat, raw poultry and dead animals.
> - Keep dogs and children from playing in sand and soil.
> - Kennel dogs on cement or gravel; avoid dirt runs.
> - Administer heartworm preventatives regularly.
> - Have your vet examine your dog's stools at your annual visits.
> - Select a boarding kennel carefully, so as to avoid contamination from other dogs or an unsanitary environment.
> - Prevent dogs from roaming. Obey local leash laws.

and then often in three months as well. Unfortunately, since dogs don't develop resistance to whipworms, it is difficult to prevent them from getting reinfected if they visit soil contaminated with whipworm eggs.

TAPEWORMS

There are many different species of tapeworm that affect dogs, but *Dipylidium caninum* is probably the most common and is spread by fleas. Flea larvae feed on organic debris and tapeworm eggs in the environment and, when a dog chews at himself and manages to ingest fleas, he might get a dose of tapeworm at the same time. The tapeworm then develops further in the intestine of the dog.

The tapeworm itself, which latches onto the intestinal wall, is composed of numerous segments. When the segments break off into the intestine (as proglottids), they may accumulate around the rectum, like grains of rice. While this tapeworm is disgusting in its behavior, it is not directly communicable to humans (although humans can also get infected by swallowing fleas).

A much more dangerous flatworm is *Echinococcus multilocularis*, which is typically found in foxes, coyotes and wolves. The eggs are passed in the feces and infect rodents, and, when dogs eat the rodents, the dogs can be infected by thousands of adult tapeworms. While the parasites don't cause many problems in dogs, this is considered the most lethal worm infection that people can get. Take appropriate precautions if you live in an area in which these tapeworms are found. Do not use mulch that may contain feces of dogs, cats or wildlife, and

discourage your pets from hunting wildlife. Treat these tapeworm infections aggressively in pets, because if humans get infected, approximately half die.

HEARTWORMS

Heartworm disease is caused by the parasite *Dirofilaria immitis* and is seen in dogs around the world. The parasite itself, another nematode, is spread between dogs by the bite of an infected mosquito. The mosquito injects infective larvae into the dog's skin with its bite, and these larvae develop under the skin for a period of time before making their way to the heart. There they develop into adults, which grow and create blockages of the heart, lungs and major blood vessels there. They also start

S. E. M. BY DR. DENNIS KUNKEL, UNIVERSITY OF HAWAII.

The dog tapeworm proglottid (body segment).

The dog tapeworm, *Taenia pisiformis*.

S. E. M. BY DR. DENNIS KUNKEL, UNIVERSITY OF HAWAII.

A Look at Internal Parasites

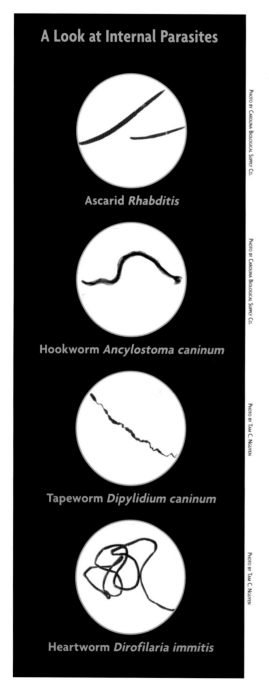

PHOTO BY CAROLINA BIOLOGICAL SUPPLY CO.

Ascarid *Rhabditis*

PHOTO BY CAROLINA BIOLOGICAL SUPPLY CO.

Hookworm *Ancylostoma caninum*

PHOTO BY TAM C. NGUYEN

Tapeworm *Dipylidium caninum*

PHOTO BY TAM C. NGUYEN

Heartworm *Dirofilaria immitis*

producing offspring (microfilariae) and these microfilariae circulate in the bloodstream, waiting to hitch a ride when the next mosquito bites. Once in the mosquito, the microfilariae develop into infective larvae and the entire process is repeated.

When dogs get infected with heartworm, over time they tend to develop symptoms associated with heart disease, such as coughing, exercise intolerance and potentially many other manifestations. Diagnosis is confirmed by either seeing the microfilariae themselves in blood samples or using immunologic tests (antigen testing) to identify the presence of adult heartworms. Since antigen tests measure the presence of adult heartworms, and microfilarial tests measure offspring produced by adults, neither are positive until six to seven months after the initial infection. However, the beginning of damage can occur by fifth-stage larvae as early as three months after infection. Thus it is possible for dogs to be harboring problem-causing larvae for up to three months before either type of test would identify an infection.

The good news is that there are great protocols available for preventing heartworm in dogs. Testing is critical in the process, and it is important to understand the benefits as well as the limitations of such testing. All dogs six months of age or older that have not been on continuous heartworm-preventive

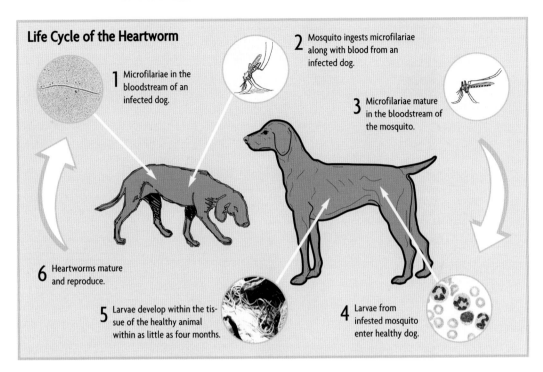

Life Cycle of the Heartworm

1 Microfilariae in the bloodstream of an infected dog.

2 Mosquito ingests microfilariae along with blood from an infected dog.

3 Microfilariae mature in the bloodstream of the mosquito.

4 Larvae from infested mosquito enter healthy dog.

5 Larvae develop within the tissue of the healthy animal within as little as four months.

6 Heartworms mature and reproduce.

medication should be screened with microfilarial or antigen tests. For dogs receiving preventive medication, periodic antigen testing helps assess the effectiveness of the preventives. The American Heartworm Society guidelines suggest that annual retesting may not be necessary when owners have absolutely provided continuous heartworm prevention. Retesting on a two- to three-year interval may be sufficient in these cases. However, your veterinarian will likely have specific guidelines under which heartworm preventives will be prescribed, and many prefer to err on the side of safety and retest annually.

It is indeed fortunate that heartworm is relatively easy to prevent, because treatments can be as life-threatening as the disease itself. Treatment requires a two-step process that kills the adult heartworms first and then the microfilariae. Prevention is obviously preferable; this involves a once-monthly oral or topical treatment. The most common oral preventives include ivermectin (not suitable for some breeds), moxidectin and milbemycin oxime; the once-a-month topical drug selamectin provides heartworm protection in addition to flea, tick and other parasite controls.

When we bring home a puppy, full of the energy and exuberance that accompanies youth, we hope for a long, happy and fulfilling relationship with the new family member. Even when we adopt an older dog, we look forward to the years of companionship ahead with a new canine friend. However, aging is inevitable for all creatures, and there will come a time when your Keeshond reaches his senior years and will need special considerations and attention to his care.

WHEN IS MY DOG A "SENIOR"?

Dogs generally are considered "seniors" at seven years of age, but that is not always accurate. A dog's senior status is better determined based on the average life expectancy for his breed, which is based on the size of the breed. A dog is considered a senior when he has reached 75% of the average lifespan for his breed. Your Keeshond has an average lifespan of 13 to 14 years and thus is a senior citizen at around 10 years of age. The Keeshond fortunately enjoys a long life, as do most members of the Spitz family. Most Keeshond

---

WEATHER WORRIES
Older pets are less tolerant of extremes in weather, both heat and cold. Your older dog should not spend extended periods in the sun; when outdoors in the warm weather, make sure he does not become overheated. In chilly weather, consider a sweater for your Kees when outdoors and limit time spent outside. Whether or not his coat is thinning, he will need provisions to keep him warm when the weather is cold. You may even place his bed by a heating duct in your living room or bedroom.

---

owners have the joy of living with an active, happy senior Kees well into the teen years.

Thus the old "seven dog years to one human year" theory is not exact. In puppyhood, a dog's year is actually comparable to more than seven human years, considering the puppy's rapid growth during his first year. Then, in adulthood, the ratio decreases. Regardless, the more viable rule of thumb is that the larger the dog, the shorter his expected lifespan. Of course, this can vary among individual dogs, with many living longer than expected, which we hope is the case!

WHAT ARE THE SIGNS OF AGING?

By the time your dog has reached his senior years, you will know him very well and thus the physical and behavioral changes that accompany aging should be noticeable to you. Humans and dogs share the most obvious

physical sign of aging: gray hair! Graying often occurs first on the muzzle and face, around the eyes. Other telltale signs are the dog's overall decrease in activity. Your older dog might be more content to nap and rest, and he may not show the same old enthusiasm when it's time to play in the yard or go for a walk. Other physical signs include significant weight loss or gain; more labored movement; skin and coat problems, possibly hair loss; sight and/or hearing problems; changes in toileting habits, perhaps seeming "unhousebroken" at times; tooth decay, bad breath or other mouth problems.

There are behavioral changes that go along with aging, too. There are numerous causes for behavioral changes. Sometimes a dog's apparent confusion results from a physical change like diminished sight or hearing. If his confusion causes him to be afraid, he may act aggressively or defensively. He may sleep more frequently because his daily walks, though shorter now, tire him out. He may begin to experience separation anxiety or, conversely, become less interested in petting and attention.

There also are clinical conditions that cause behavioral changes in older dogs. One such condition is known as canine cognitive dysfunction (familiarly known as "old-dog" syndrome). It

ADAPTING TO AGE

As dogs age and their once-keen senses begin to deteriorate, they can experience stress and confusion. However, dogs are very adaptable and most can adjust to deficiencies in their sight and hearing. As these processes often deteriorate gradually, the dog makes adjustments gradually, too. Because dogs become so familiar with the layout of their homes and yards, and with their daily routines, they are able to get around even if they cannot see or hear as well. Help your senior dog by keeping things consistent around the house. Keep up with your regular times for walking and potty trips, and do not relocate his crate or rearrange the furniture. Your dog is a very adaptable creature and can make compensation for his diminished ability, but you want to help him along the way and not make changes that will cause him confusion.

can be frustrating for an owner whose dog is affected with cognitive dysfunction, as it can result in behavioral changes of all types, most seemingly unexplainable. Common changes include the dog's forgetting aspects of the daily routine, such as times to eat, go out for walks, relieve himself and the like. Along the same lines, you may take your dog out at the regular time for a potty trip and he may have no idea why he is there. Sometimes a placid dog will begin to show aggressive or possessive tendencies or, conversely, a hyperactive dog will start to "mellow out."

Disease also can be the cause of behavioral changes in senior dogs. Hormonal problems (Cushing's disease is common in older dogs), diabetes and thyroid disease can cause increased appetite, which can lead to aggression related to food guarding. It's better to be proactive with your senior dog, making more frequent trips to the vet if necessary and having bloodwork done to test for the diseases that can commonly befall older dogs.

This is not to say that, as dogs age, they all fall apart physically and become nasty in personality. The aforementioned changes are discussed to alert owners to the things that may happen as their dogs get older. Many hardy dogs remain active and alert well into old age. However, it can be

frustrating and heartbreaking for owners to see their beloved dogs change physically and temperamentally. Just know that it's the same Keeshond under there and that he still loves you and appreciates your care, which he needs now more than ever.

HOW DO I CARE FOR MY AGING DOG?

Again, every dog is an individual in terms of aging. Your dog might reach the estimated "senior" age for his breed and show no signs of slowing down. However, even if he shows no outward signs of aging, he should begin a senior-care program once he reaches the determined age. He may not show it, but he's not a pup anymore! By providing him with extra attention to his veterinary care at this age, you will be practicing good preventive medicine, ensuring that the rest of your dog's life will be as long, active, happy and healthy as possible. If you do notice indications of aging, such as graying and/or changes in sleeping, eating or toileting habits, this is a sign to set up a senior-care visit with your vet right away to make sure that these changes are not related to any health problems.

To start, senior dogs should visit the vet twice yearly for exams, routine tests and overall evaluations. Many veterinarians have special screening programs especially for senior dogs that can include a thorough physical exam; blood test to determine complete blood count; serum biochemistry test, which screens for liver, kidney and blood problems as well as cancer; urinalysis; and dental exams. With these tests, it can be determined if your dog has any health problems; the results also establish a baseline for your pet against which future test results can be compared.

In addition to these tests, your vet may suggest additional testing, including an EKG, tests for glaucoma and other problems of the eye, chest X-rays, screening for tumors, blood pressure test, test for thyroid function and screening for parasites and reassessment of his preventative program. Your vet also will ask you questions about your dog's diet and activity level, what you feed and the amounts that you feed. This information, along with his evaluation of the dog's overall condition, will enable him to suggest proper dietary changes, if needed.

This may seem like quite a work-up for your pet, but veterinarians advise that older dogs need more frequent attention so that any health problems can be detected as early as possible. Serious conditions like kidney disease, heart disease and cancer may not present outward symptoms, or the problem may go

COPING WITH A BLIND DOG
Blindness is one of the unfortunate realities of growing old, for both dogs and humans. Owners of blind dogs should not give up hope, as most dogs adapt to their compromised state with grace and patience. A sudden loss of sight poses more stress on the dog than a gradual loss, such as that through cataracts. Some dogs may need your assistance to help them get around; others will move around seemingly uninhibited. Owners may need to retrain the dog to handle some basic tasks. Teaching commands like "Wait," "Stop" and "Slow" are handy as you help the dog learn to maneuver around his world. You are now more than the team captain, you're the coach and cheerleader! If your blind dog is showing signs of depression, it is your job to encourage him and give him moral support, just as you might for a member of your family or a good friend.

undetected if the symptoms are mistaken by owners as just part of the aging process.

There are some conditions more common in elderly dogs that are difficult to ignore. Cognitive dysfunction shares much in common with senility and Alzheimer's disease, and dogs are not immune. Dogs can become confused and/or disoriented, lose their house-training, have abnormal sleep-wake cycles and interact differently with their owners. Be heartened by the fact that, in some ways, there are more treatment options for dogs with cognitive dysfunction than for people with similar conditions. There is good evidence that continued stimulation in the form of games, play, training and exercise can help to maintain cognitive function. There are also medications (such as seligiline) and antioxidant-fortified senior diets that have been shown to be beneficial.

Cancer is also a condition more common in the elderly. Almost all of the cancers seen in people are also seen in pets. While we can't control the effects of second-hand smoke, lung cancer, which is a major killer in humans, is relatively rare in dogs. If pets are getting regular physical examinations, cancers are often detected early. There are a variety of cancer therapies available today and many pets continue to live happy lives with appropriate treatment.

Degenerative joint disease, often referred to as arthritis, is another common malady shared between elderly dogs and humans. A lifetime of wear and tear on joints, and running around at play, eventually takes its toll and results in stiffness and difficulty getting around. As dogs live longer and healthier lives, it is natural that they should eventually feel some of the effects of aging. Once again, if regular veterinary care has been available,

WHEN IS YOUR DOG A GERIATRIC?

A survey of the diplomates of the American Board of Veterinary Practicioners and the American Colleges of Veterinary Internal Medicine, Veterinary Surgery and the Veterinary Pathologists defined a "geriatric" dog as one who begins to experience age-related health problems. The age at which to consider a dog geriatric is based on the dog's size. Small dogs, those that weigh 20 lbs or less, would be considered geriatric at around 12 years of age. Medium dogs, from 21 to 50 lbs, are geriatric at 10 years of age. Large dogs, from 51 to 90 lbs, at about 9 years of age. Giant dogs, those over 90 lbs, at about 8 years of age. These ages vary, of course, with individual dogs and breeds.

> ## ACCIDENT ALERT!
> Just as we puppy-proof our homes for the new member of the family, we must accident-proof our homes for the older dog. You want to create a safe environment in which the senior dog can get around easily and comfortably, with no dangers. A dog that slips and falls in old age is much more prone to injury than an adult, making accident prevention even more important. Likewise, dogs are more prone to falls in old age, as they do not have the same balance and coordination that they once had. Throw rugs on hardwood floors are slippery and pose a risk; even a throw rug on a carpeted surface be an obstacle for the senior dog. Consider putting down non-slip surfaces or confining your dog to carpeted rooms only.

your pet was not carrying extra pounds all those years and wearing those joints out before their time. If your pet was unfortunate enough to inherit hip dysplasia, osteochondrosis dissecans, or any of the other developmental orthopedic diseases, battling the onset of degenerative joint disease was probably a longstanding goal. In any case, there are now many effective remedies for managing degenerative joint disease and a number of remarkable surgeries as well.

Aside from the extra veterinary care, there is much you can do at home to keep your older dog in good condition. The dog's diet is an important factor. If your dog's appetite decreases, he will not be getting the nutrients he needs. He also will lose weight, which is unhealthy for a dog at a proper weight. Conversely, an older dog's metabolism is slower

and he usually exercises less, but he should not be allowed to become obese. Obesity in an older dog is especially risky, because extra pounds mean extra stress on the body, increasing his vulnerability to heart disease. Plus, the additional pounds make it harder for the dog to move about.

You should discuss age-related feeding changes with your vet. For a dog who has lost interest in food, it may be suggested to try some different types of food until you find something new that the dog likes. For an obese dog, a "light" formula dog food or reducing food portions may be advised, along with exercise appropriate to his physical condition and energy level.

As for exercise, despite his old age, the senior dog should not be allowed to become a "couch potato." He may not be able to handle the morning run, long

Number-One Killer Disease in Dogs: CANCER

In every age, there is a word associated with a disease or plague that causes humans to shudder. In the 21st century, that word is "cancer." Just as cancer is the leading cause of death in humans, it claims nearly half the lives of dogs that die from a natural disease as well as half the dogs that die over the age of ten years.

Described as a genetic disease, cancer becomes a greater risk as the dog ages. Vets and dog owners have become increasingly aware of the threat of cancer to dogs. Statistics reveal that one dog in every five will develop cancer, the most common of which is skin cancer. Many cancers, including prostate, ovarian and breast cancer, can be avoided by spaying and neutering our dogs by the age of six months.

Early detection of cancer can save or extend a dog's life, so it is absolutely vital for owners to have their dogs examined by a qualified vet or oncologist immediately upon detection of any abnormality. Certain dietary guidelines have also proven to reduce the onset and spread of cancer. Foods based on fish rather than beef, due to the presence of Omega-3 fatty acids, are recommended. Other amino acids such as glutamine have significant benefits for canines, particularly those breeds that show a greater susceptibility to cancer.

Cancer management and treatments promise hope for future generations of canines. Since the disease is genetic, breeders should never breed a dog whose parents, grandparents and any related siblings have developed cancer. It is difficult to know whether to exclude an otherwise healthy dog from a breeding program, as the disease does not manifest itself until the dog's senior years.

RECOGNIZE CANCER WARNING SIGNS

Since early detection can possibly rescue your dog from becoming a cancer statistic, it is essential for owners to recognize the possible signs and seek the assistance of a qualified professional.

- Abnormal bumps or lumps that continue to grow
- Bleeding or discharge from any body cavity
- Persistent stiffness or lameness
- Recurrent sores or sores that do not heal
- Inappetence
- Breathing difficulties
- Weight loss
- Bad breath or odors
- General malaise and fatigue
- Eating and swallowing problems
- Difficulty urinating and defecating

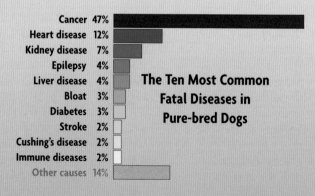

Cancer	47%
Heart disease	12%
Kidney disease	7%
Epilepsy	4%
Liver disease	4%
Bloat	3%
Diabetes	3%
Stroke	2%
Cushing's disease	2%
Immune diseases	2%
Other causes	14%

The Ten Most Common Fatal Diseases in Pure-bred Dogs

walks and vigorous games of fetch, but he still needs to get up and get moving. Keep up with your daily walks, but keep the distances shorter, and let your dog set the pace. If he gets to the point where he's not up for walks, let him stroll around the yard. On the other hand, many dogs remain very active in their senior years, so base changes to the exercise program on your own individual dog and what he's capable of. Don't worry, your Kees will let you know when it's time to rest.

Keep up with your grooming routine as you always have. Be extra diligent about checking the skin and coat for problems. Older dogs can experience thinning coats as a normal aging process, but they can also lose hair as a result of medical problems. Some thinning is normal, but patches of baldness or the loss of significant amounts of hair is not.

Hopefully, you've been regular with brushing your dog's teeth throughout his life. Healthy teeth directly affect overall good health. We already know that bacteria from gum infections can enter the dog's body through the damaged gums and travel to the organs. At a stage in life when his organs don't function as well as they used to, you don't want anything to put additional strain on them. Clean teeth also contribute to a healthy immune system. Offering the dental-type chews in addition to toothbrushing can help, as they remove plaque and tartar as the dog chews.

Along with the same good care you've given him all of his life, pay a little extra attention to your dog in his senior years and keep up with twice-yearly trips to the vet. The sooner a problem is uncovered, the greater the chances of a full recovery.

SAYING GOODBYE

While you can help your dog live as long a life as possible, you can't help him life forever. A dog's lifespan is short when compared to that of a human, so it is inevitable that pet owners will experience loss. To many, losing a beloved dog is like losing a family member. Our dogs are part of our lives every day; they are our true loyal friends and always seem to know when it's time to comfort us, to celebrate with us or to just provide the company of a caring friend. Even if we know that our dog is nearing his final days, we can never quite prepare for his being gone.

Many dogs live out long lives and simply die of old age. Others unfortunately are taken suddenly by illness or accident, and still others find their senior years compromised by disease and physical problems. In some of these cases, owners find themselves having to make difficult decisions.

Is dog showing in your blood? Are you excited by the idea of gaiting your handsome Keeshond around the ring to the thunderous applause of an enthusiastic audience? Are you certain that your beloved Keeshond is flawless? You are not alone! Every loving owner thinks that his dog has no faults, or too few to mention. No matter how many times an owner reads over the breed standard, he cannot find any faults in his aristocratic companion dog. If this sounds like you, and if you are considering entering your Keeshond in a dog show, here are some basic questions to ask yourself:

• Did you purchase a "show-quality" puppy from the breeder?
• Is your puppy at least six months of age?
• Does the puppy exhibit correct show type for his breed?
• Does your puppy have any disqualifying faults?
• Is your Keeshond registered with the American Kennel Club?
• How much time do you have to devote to training, grooming, conditioning and exhibiting your dog?
• Do you understand the rules and regulations of a dog show?
• Do you have time to learn how to show your dog properly?
• Do you have the financial resources to invest in showing your dog?
• Will you show the dog yourself or hire a professional handler?
• Do you have a vehicle that can accommodate your weekend trips to the dog shows?

Success in the show ring requires more than a pretty face, a waggy tail and a pocketful of liver. Even though dog shows can be exciting and enjoyable, the sport of conformation makes great demands on the exhibitors and the dogs. Winning exhibitors live for their dogs, devoting time and money to their dogs' presentation, conditioning and training. Very few novices, even those with good dogs, will find themselves in the winners' circle, though it does happen. Don't be disheartened, though. Every exhibitor began as a novice and worked his way up to the Group ring. It's the "working your way up" part that you must keep in mind.

Assuming that you have purchased a puppy of the correct type and quality for showing, let's begin to examine the world of showing and what's required to get started. Although the entry fee into a dog show is nominal, there are lots of other hidden costs involved with "finishing" your Keeshond, that is, making him a champion. Things like equipment, travel, training and conditioning all cost money. A more serious campaign will include fees for a professional handler, boarding, cross-country travel and advertising. Top-winning show dogs can represent a very considerable investment—over $100,000 has been spent in campaigning some dogs. (The investment can be less, of course, for owners who don't use professional handlers.)

Many owners, on the other hand, enter their "average" Keeshonds in dog shows for the fun and enjoyment of it. Dog showing makes an absorbing hobby, with many rewards for dogs and owners alike. If you're having fun, meeting other people who share your interests and enjoying the overall experience, you likely will catch the "bug." Once the dog-show bug bites, its effects can last a lifetime; it's certainly much better than a deer tick! Soon you will be envisioning yourself in the center ring at the

---

FOR MORE INFORMATION....

For reliable up-to-date information about registration, dog shows and other canine competitions, contact one of the national registries by mail or via the Internet.

American Kennel Club
5580 Centerview Dr., Raleigh, NC 27606-3390
www.akc.org

United Kennel Club
100 E. Kilgore Road, Kalamazoo, MI 49002
www.ukcdogs.com

Canadian Kennel Club
89 Skyway Ave., Suite 100, Etobicoke, Ontario
M9W 6R4 Canada
www.ckc.ca

The Kennel Club
1-5 Clarges St., Piccadilly, London W1Y 8AB, UK
www.the-kennel-club.org.uk

Westminster Kennel Club Dog Show in New York City, competing for the prestigious Best in Show cup. This magical dog show is televised annually from Madison Square Garden, and the victorious dog becomes a celebrity overnight.

AKC CONFORMATION SHOWING

GETTING STARTED

Visiting a dog show as a spectator is a great place to start. Pick up the show catalog to find out what time your breed is being shown, who is judging the breed and in what ring the classes will be held. To start, Keeshonds compete against other Keeshonds, and the winner is selected as Best of Breed by the judge. This is the procedure for each breed. At a group show, all of the Best of Breed winners go on to compete for Group One in their respective Group. For example, all Best of Breed winners for any given Group compete against each other; this is done for all seven groups. Finally, all seven group winners go head to head in the ring for the Best in Show award.

What most spectators don't understand is the basic idea of conformation. A dog show is often referred as a "conformation" show. This means that the judge should decide how each dog stacks up (conforms) to the breed standard for his given breed: how well does this Keeshond conform to the ideal representative detailed in the standard? Ideally, this is what happens. In reality, however, this ideal often gets slighted as the judge compares Keeshond #1 to Keeshond #2. Again, the ideal is that each dog is judged based on his merits in comparison to his breed standard, not in comparison to the other dogs in the ring. It is easier for judges to compare dogs of the same breed to decide which they think is the better specimen; in the Group and Best in Show ring, however, it is very difficult to compare one breed to another, like apples to oranges. Thus, the dog's conformation to the breed standard is essential to his success. Good handling and advertising dollars also count.

The breed standard, which is drafted and approved by the breed's national parent club, the Keeshond Club of America, has been approved by the American Kennel Club (AKC). The dog described in the standard is the perfect dog of that breed, and breeders keep their eye on the standard when they choose which dogs to breed, hoping to get closer and closer to the ideal with each litter.

Another good first step for the novice is to join a dog club. You will be astonished by the many and different kinds of dog clubs in the country, with about 5,000

Dog shows are competitive events where good showmanship, responsible breeding and a little bit of luck are the winners of the day.

clubs holding events every year. Most clubs require that prospective new members present two letters of recommendation from existing members. Perhaps you've made some friends visiting a show held by a particular club and you would like to join that club. Dog clubs may specialize in a single breed, like a local or regional Keeshond club, or in a specific pursuit, such as obedience, tracking or hunting tests. There are all-breed clubs for all dog enthusiasts, which sponsor special training days, seminars on topics like grooming or handling or lectures on breeding or canine genetics. There are also clubs that specialize in certain types of dogs, like herding dogs, hunting dogs, companion dogs, etc.

A parent club is the national organization, sanctioned by the AKC, which promotes and safeguards its breed in the country. The Keeshond Club of America can be contacted on the Internet at www.keeshond.org. The parent club holds an annual national specialty show, usually in a different city each year, in which many of the country's top dogs, handlers and breeders gather to compete. At a specialty show, only members of a single breed are invited to participate. There are also group specialties, in which all members of a Group are invited. For more information

SEAL OF EXCELLENCE

The show ring is the testing ground for a breeder's program. A championship on a dog signifies that three qualified judges have placed their seal of approval on a dog. Only dogs that have earned their championships should be considered for breeding purposes. Striving to improve the breed and reproduce sound, typical examples of the breed, breeders must breed only the best. No breeder breeds only for pet homes; they strive for the top. The goal of every program must be to better the breed, and every responsible breeder wants the prestige of producing Best in Show winners.

about dog clubs in your area, contact the AKC at www.akc.org on the Internet or write them at their Raleigh, NC address.

HOW SHOWS ARE ORGANIZED

Three kinds of conformation shows are offered by the AKC. There is the all-breed show, in which all AKC-recognized breeds can compete; the specialty show, which is for one breed only and usually sponsored by the breed's parent club and the group show, for all breeds in one of the seven AKC groups. The Keeshond competes in the Non-Sporting Group.

For a dog to become an AKC champion of record, the dog must earn 15 points at shows. The points must be awarded by at least three different judges and must include two "majors" under different judges. A "major" is a three-, four- or five-point win, and the number of points per win is determined by the number of dogs competing in the show on that day. Dogs that are absent or are excused are not counted. The number of points that are awarded varies from breed to breed. More dogs are needed to attain a major in more popular breeds, and fewer dogs are needed in less popular breeds. Yearly, the AKC evaluates the number of dogs in competition in each division (there are 14 divisions in all, based on geography) and may or may not change the numbers of dogs required for each number of points. For example, a major in Division 2 (Delaware, New Jersey and Pennsylvania) recently required 17 dogs or 16 bitches for a three-point major, 29 dogs or 27 bitches for a four-point major and 51 dogs or 46 bitches for a five-point major. The Keeshond attracts fairly good numbers at all-breed shows, though not as many as popular breeds like the Poodle or Labrador Retriever.

Only one dog and one bitch of each breed can win points at a given show. There are no "co-ed" classes except for champions of record. Dogs and bitches do not compete against each other until they are champions. Dogs that are not champions (referred to as "class dogs") compete in one of five classes. The class in which a dog is entered depends on age and previous show wins. First there is the Puppy Class (sometimes divided further into classes for 6- to 9-month-olds and 9- to 12-month-olds); next is the Novice Class (for dogs that have no points toward their championship and whose only first-place wins have come in the Puppy Class or the Novice Class, the latter class limited to three first places); then there is the American-bred Class (for dogs bred in the US); the Bred-by-Exhibitor Class (for dogs handled by their breeders or by immediate family members of their breeders) and the Open Class (for any non-champions). Any dog may enter the Open class, regardless of age or win history, but to be competi-

DRESS THE PART

It's a dog show, so don't forget your costume. Even though the show is about the dog, you also must play your role well. You have been cast as the "dog handler" and you must smartly dress the part. Solid colors make a nice complement to the dog's coat, and choose colors that contrast. You don't want to be wearing an essentially gray outfit that matches the color of your essentially gray Keeshond. Whether the show is indoors or out, you still must dress properly. You want the judge to perceive you as professional, so polish, polish, polish! And don't forget to wear sensible shoes; remember, you have to gait around the ring with your dog.

tive the dog should be older and have ring experience.

The judge at the show begins judging the male dogs in the Puppy Class(es) and proceeds through the classes. The judge awards first through fourth place in each class. The first-place winners of each class then compete with one another in the Winners Class to determine Winners Dog. The judge then starts over with the bitches, beginning with the Puppy Class(es) and proceeding up to the Winners Class to award Winners Bitch, just as he did with the dogs. A Reserve Winners Dog and Reserve Winners Bitch are also selected; they could be awarded the points in the case of a disqualification.

The Winners Dog and Winners Bitch are the two that are awarded the points for their breed. They then go on to compete with any champions of record (often called "specials") of their breed that are entered in the show. The champions may be dogs or bitches; in this class, all are shown together. The judge reviews the Winners Dog and Winners Bitch along with all of the champions to select the Best of Breed winner. The Best of Winners is selected between the Winners Dog and Winners Bitch; if one of these two is selected Best of Breed as well, he or she is automatically determined Best of Winners. Lastly, the judge selects Best of Opposite Sex to the Best of Breed winner. The Best of Breed winner then goes on to the Group competition.

At a Group or all-breed show, the Best of Breed winners from each breed are divided into their respective groups to compete against one another for Group One through Group Four. Group One (first place) is awarded to the dog that best lives up to the ideal for his breed as described in the standard. A Group judge, therefore, must have a thorough working knowledge of many breed standards. After placements have been made in each Group,

MEET THE AKC

The American Kennel Club is the main governing body of the dog sport in the United States. Founded in 1884, the AKC consists of 500 or more independent dog clubs plus 4,500 affiliated clubs, all of which follow the AKC rules and regulations. Additionally, the AKC maintains a registry for pure-bred dogs in the US and works to preserve the integrity of the sport and its continuation in the country. Over 1,000,000 dogs are registered each year, representing about 150 recognized breeds. There are over 15,000 competitive events held annually for which over 2,000,000 dogs enter to participate. Dogs compete to earn over 40 different titles, from Champion to Companion Dog to Master Agility Champion.

Your Keeshond must be six months of age or older and registered with the AKC in order to be entered in AKC-sanctioned shows in which there are classes for the Keeshond. Your Keeshond also must not possess any disqualifying faults and must be sexually intact. The reason for the latter is simple: dog shows are the proving grounds to determine which dogs and bitches are worthy of being bred. If they cannot be bred, that defeats the purpose! On that note, only dogs that have achieved championships, thus proving their excellent quality, should be bred. If you have spayed or neutered your dog, however, there are many AKC events other than conformation, such as obedience trials, agility trials and the Canine Good Citizen® program, in which you and your Keeshond can participate.

the seven Group One winners (from the Sporting Group, Toy Group, Hound Group, etc.) compete against each other for the top honor, Best in Show.

There are different ways to find out about dog shows in your area. The American Kennel Club's monthly magazine, the *American Kennel Gazette,* is accompanied by the *Events Calendar;* this magazine is available through subscription. You can also look on the AKC's and your parent club's websites for information, and check the event listings in your local newspaper.

OTHER TYPES OF COMPETITION

OBEDIENCE TRIALS

Mrs. Helen Whitehouse Walker, a Standard Poodle fancier, can be credited with introducing obedience trials to the United States. In the 1930s she designed a series of exercises based on those of the Associated Sheep, Police, Army Dog Society of Great Britain. These exercises were intended to evaluate the working relationship between dog and owner. Since those early days of the sport in the US, obedience trials have grown more and more popular, and now more than 2,000 trials each year attract over 100,000 dogs and their owners. Any dog registered with the AKC, regardless of neutering or other disqualifications that would preclude his entry in conformation competition, can participate in obedience trials.

There are three levels of difficulty in obedience competition. The first (and easiest) level is the Novice, in which dogs can earn the Companion Dog (CD) title. The intermediate level is the Open level, in which the Companion Dog Excellent (CDX) title is awarded. The advanced level is the Utility level, in which dogs compete for the Utility Dog

(UD) title. Classes at each level are further divided into "A" and "B," with "A" for beginners and "B" for those with more experience. In order to win a title at a given level, a dog must earn three "legs." A "leg" is accomplished when a dog scores 170 or higher (200 is a perfect score). The scoring system gets a little trickier when you understand that a dog must score more than 50% of the points available for each exercise in order to actually earn the points. Available points for each exercise range between 20 and 40.

A dog must complete different exercises at each level of obedience. The Novice exercises are the easiest, with the Open and finally the Utility levels progressing in difficulty. Examples of Novice exercises are on- and off-lead heeling, a figure-8 pattern,

How exhilarating to see a Keeshond and his owner cooperate so closely, running side by side, in an agility competition!

performing a recall (or come), long sit and long down and standing for examination. In the Open level, the Novice-level exercises are required again, but this time without a leash and for longer durations. In addition, the dog must clear a broad jump, retrieve over a jump and drop on recall. In the Utility level, the exercises are quite difficult, including executing basic commands based on hand signals, following a heeling pattern, locating articles based on scent discrimination and completing jumps at the handler's direction.

Once he's earned the UD title, a dog can go on to win the prestigious title of Utility Dog Excellent (UDX) by winning "legs" in ten shows. Additionally, Utility Dogs who win "legs" in Open B and Utility B earn points toward the lofty title of Obedience Trial Champion (OTCh.). Established in 1977 by the AKC, this title requires a dog to earn 100 points as well as three first places in a combination of Open B and Utility B classes under three different judges. The "brass ring" of obedience competition is the AKC's National Obedience Invitational. This is an exclusive competition for only the cream of the obedience crop. In order to qualify for the invitational, a dog must be either ranked in the top 25 all-breeds in obedience or be ranked in the top three for his breed in obedience. The title at stake here is that of National Obedience Champion (NOC).

AGILITY TRIALS

Agility trials became sanctioned by the AKC in August 1994, when the first licensed agility trials were held. Since that time, agility certainly has grown in popularity by leaps and bounds, literally! The AKC allows all registered breeds (including Miscellaneous Class breeds) to participate, providing the dog is 12 months of age or older. Agility is designed so that the handler demonstrates how well the dog can work at his side. The handler directs his dog through, over, under and around an obstacle course that includes jumps, tires, the dog walk, weave poles, pipe tunnels, collapsed tunnels and more. While working his way through the course, the dog must keep one eye and ear on the handler and the rest of his body on the course. The handler runs along with the dog, giving verbal and hand signals to guide the dog through the course.

The first organization to promote agility trials in the US was the United States Dog Agility Association, Inc. (USDAA). Established in 1986, the USDAA sparked the formation of many member clubs around the country. To participate in USDAA trials, dogs must be at least 18 months of age.

The USDAA and AKC both offer titles to winning dogs, although the exercises and requirements of the two organizations differ. Agility Dog (AD), Advanced Agility Dog (AAD) and Master Agility Dog (MAD) are the titles offered by the USDAA, while the AKC offers Novice Agility (NA), Open Agility (OA), Agility Excellent (AX) and Master Agility Excellent (MX). Beyond these four AKC titles, dogs can win additional titles in "jumper" classes: Jumper with Weave Novice (NAJ), Open (OAJ) and Excellent (MXJ). The ultimate title in AKC agility is MACH, Master Agility Champion. Dogs can continue to add number designations to the MACH title, indicating how many times the dog has met the title's requirements (MACH1, MACH2 and so on).

Agility trials are a great way to keep your dog active, and they will keep you running, too! You should join a local agility club to learn more about the sport. These clubs offer sessions in which you can introduce your dog to the various obstacles as well as training classes to prepare him for competition. In no time, your dog will be climbing A-frames, crossing the dog walk and flying over hurdles, all with you right beside him. Your heart will leap every time your dog jumps through the hoop—and you'll be

having just as much (if not more) fun!

The bottom line is this: There is so much to do with your dog that it can be hard to decide which event to try! Just as we have to choose what to do with our weekends, so do the dogs. Whatever you choose to do with your Keeshond, it will take training, dedication and a willingness to work with your dog to achieve a common goal, a partnership between the two of you. There is nothing more pleasing than to watch a handler and dog performing at a high level, whether it is in the show ring or the field. There is something for everyone and every dog in the world of dog "showing." Dog showing should really be called "competing with your dog." You are not restricted to the traditional "dog show" and may find that your "show dog" excels in other areas as well or instead.

At an FCI show, the group judging for Group 5, Spitz and Primitive-type dogs, is underway.

INDEX

My Keeshond

PUT YOUR PUPPY'S FIRST PICTURE HERE

Dog's Name _____

Date _____ Photographer _____